ALFRED GILBEY

ALFRED GILBEY

A MEMOIR BY SOME FRIENDS

Edited by David Watkin

MICHAEL RUSSELL

© Contributors as named 2001

First published in Great Britain 2001
by Michael Russell (Publishing) Ltd
Wilby Hall, Wilby, Norwich NR16 2JP

Typeset in Sabon by Waveney Typesetters
Wymondham, Norfolk
Printed and bound in Great Britain
by Biddles Ltd, Guildford and King's Lynn

ISBN 0 85955 270 5

Contents

Introduction

The age of the thirteen contributors to this book ranged at the time of writing from twenty-three to ninety-three. It seems particularly happy that the two youngest contributors, Hugh-Guy Lorriman and Charles des Forges, who both helped tend Alfred towards the end of his life, are sons of close friends of his, Nicholas Lorriman and John des Forges. This is a clear indication of the way in which Alfred's eternal youthfulness of mind and spirit enabled him to make new and close friends at an advanced age.

The contributors also reflect something of the wide range of his interests, first and foremost his religion: hence the choice of Father Ronald Creighton-Jobe, a priest of the Oratory, an institution which owed much to the numerous young men whom Alfred successfully encouraged to try their vocation there. Nine of the contributors were educated at Cambridge, where seven of them had the good fortune to be members of his flock at Fisher House. This also seems appropriate as an indication of the centrality of Cambridge to Alfred's affections and mission. Peter Gregory-Jones, author of *A History of the Cambridge Catholic Chaplaincy 1895–1965* (1986), knows more than anyone else about Alfred's life as chaplain at Fisher House.

Alfred's love of hunting, first the fox and later the hare, is shared by at least four of the other contributors: Major-General the Viscount Monckton of Brenchley, Stephen Lambert, Master of the Trinity Foot Beagles, Lord Patten, sometime Secretary of State for Education, and Nicholas Lorriman, a Lecturer at the Sorbonne. Alfred's cousin, Jack Gold, has contributed a piece on Mark Hall, Alfred's beloved family home in Essex, long destroyed but a central pivot in his life. Charles Hargrove, former Paris correspondent of *The Times*, shared his interest in the history of ideas. Professor

Jocelyn Hillgarth is a patristic scholar. Mark Bence-Jones is a prolific author of books, many on social history which was always a central passion for Alfred. Finally, my own role as a Fellow of Peterhouse and an architectural historian was welcomed by Alfred who loved the ancient colleges of Cambridge as well as the history of architecture of which he had a detailed knowledge.

There are, of course, many other aspects of Alfred's life and enthusiasms which could have featured more strongly: these include literature and especially poetry, of which he could quote much by heart, and also heraldry which rivalled only architecture in his affections. No less importantly, there are many other close friends of Alfred who could equally well have contributed to this book. However, the greatest gap, as Jocelyn Hillgarth points out in his contribution, is the result of the fact that because Alfred lived so long, 'he was predeceased by nearly all those who had known him when he was young'. How wonderful it would have been, Jocelyn speculates, to have had contributions from Alfred's Oxford friends such as Ronald Knox and David and Gervase Mathew.

In the end, all would agree that Alfred is chiefly remembered not as a herald, still less a foxhunter, but as someone who both gave and received more love than anyone they have ever been privileged to know.

D. J. W.

Mark Bence-Jones

SOME MEMORIES OF ALFRED GILBEY

I had the good fortune to know Alfred Gilbey for half a century; a half-century that began when I went up to Cambridge where Alfred was then Catholic Chaplain to the University. As a Catholic I naturally got to know the Catholic Chaplain; but Alfred Gilbey soon came to play a far greater part in my Cambridge life – as he did in the lives of so many of my fellow-undergraduates – than any Chaplain, however admirable, would normally have done. In fact he took the place of one of those legendary dons who loom so large in the undergraduate memory of previous generations – 'Sligger' Urquhart at Oxford, for example. One had looked forward to meeting dons of this sort but they turned out to be rather thin on the ground in the Cambridge of the late 1940s. They still existed but they seldom came the way of undergraduates like myself. The dons who associated with the likes of me were worthy and proficient in their subjects without quite measuring up to one's idea of an eminent Cambridge don. But one person who really did measure up to that idea was Alfred Gilbey.

Strictly speaking he was not a don, not being a Fellow of any college. But he was of our parents' generation and a senior member of the University, a graduate of Trinity; though he had only got a pass degree – euphemistically called a 'Special' – and had taken four years to get it. But if in what he liked to call his 'mis-spent youth' he had neglected his studies, he had made up for this neglect in later years by reading and in other ways, so that by the time I knew him he was a most highly educated and well-read person; without being in any way a pedant. In particular his knowledge of the history of Cambridge and its lore was without equal.

Alfred's dress – the frock coat, the broad-brimmed or tall hat, the cassock trimmed with purple after he became a Domestic Prelate to the Pope in 1950 – seemed to convey something of the sartorial formality associated with a high university dignitary, though very much more elegant. In the same way, Fisher House, the Catholic Chaplaincy, in Alfred's day had very much the air of a Cambridge college: the court, small as it was, the panelled dining room hung with portraits, the Great Chamber upstairs with its books and its blazing fire. Here, as an undergraduate, one would drop in uninvited and be given the warmest of welcomes; together with a glass of sherry or port if the hour was appropriate. Years later, when Alfred was living at the Travellers' Club, he offered me some port of the kind he had given us at Cambridge. The family wine firm no longer supplied it; but his cousin who ran the firm had unexpectedly come upon some bottles. I was amazed by how good it was. 'Is this really the port which we drank every evening when we came to see you as undergraduates?' I asked. 'My father used to bring it on picnics' Alfred replied. 'He used to say "It's water, dear boy, just water."'

Drinking port with me on another occasion, Alfred came out with a memorable quotation from some long-forgotten eighteenth-century ecclesiastical memoirs.

'Shall I open another bottle of claret, Mr Dean?' asked his courteous host.

'I should not object to another bottle, or even two' replied the Dean. 'But I should warn you, I have so weak a stomach, it is my custom at this hour of the night to drink out a bottle of port.'

The port and the sherry were a major contribution to the pleasant country house atmosphere of the Chaplaincy. It was a very well-run country house; for Alfred, in domestic matters, was punctilious. For example, he always had a bowl of hot water on his breakfast table to keep the butter knife warm so that it would cut all the more easily through the butter.

Alfred's fund of quotations and anecdotes, combined with his friendliness and charm, made him the wonderful company he was. He also had the rare talent of being extremely witty about people without being uncharitable. During the fifty years that I knew him, I can only remember his being uncharitable twice. The first time was when he said of a Cambridge contemporary of mine whom I had always thought of as a rather saintly person, 'He's so polite I always think he'd make a perfect undertaker.' The second time was many years later at the Travellers' Club; I can remember the actual place where he made the uncharitable remark but I cannot remember what it was.

In conversation, Alfred was a stickler for correct usage. Thus he would maintain that the only things it was permissible to take were medicine and offence; it was not correct to speak of taking a bath. And while he was in no way a prude, he avoided improprieties if he possibly could; and if obliged to say something improper he would couch it in terms suitable for what he regarded as polite society. He once came up to me in a room at Fisher House in which he had recently hung a set of early nineteenth-century satirical prints of the various ways in which a Cambridge freshman could annoy the authorities; I was looking at one in which the freshman was committing the offence of using what the caption termed 'The Fellows' bog'. 'Ah, you're looking at the one of him using the Fellows' rears' Alfred said, paraphrasing a rather vulgar slang expression with a piece of more acceptable slang. The term he used was in no way genteel; it was, as he once said in another context, 'smoking room rather than tap room.'

While more often than not we visited Alfred Gilbey for worldly reasons and while indeed many of those who frequented Fisher House were not even members of his flock, one never forgot that he was Chaplain. It was not that religion featured to any great extent in his conversation – far from it; but one was always aware of his piety and his rock-like faith. To him, loss of faith or lack of it was the greatest of all misfortunes. He once told me of how he had never forgotten an episode of his childhood or early boyhood in Essex. His parents were commiserating with the local Anglican clergyman whose wife had just died. 'Yes' said the clergyman sadly. 'It's such a snuffing out.' For the rest of his long life, Alfred, who believed so strongly in the next world, felt sorry for that clergyman.

Because as Chaplain Alfred Gilbey instructed many converts to Catholicism, the myth grew up that he set out to make converts. In fact he never proselytised; his so-called converts had already made up their mind that they wished to become Catholics by the time they came to him for instruction; most of them when they came for instruction had never met him before. The non-Catholic undergraduates with whom he associated tended to be young men keen on hunting and not much given to religious discussion; many of them became his lifelong friends, while never having any leanings towards Catholicism.

Insofar as Alfred can be said to have 'made' converts, this was simply by his example: his kindness and his serenity and the way in which he combined otherworldliness with a deep interest in and knowledge of this world. And while he was obviously well prepared for death, he enjoyed life to the full. Perhaps the nearest Alfred can be said to have come to proselytising was by showing Catholicism in an attractive light; though at times he did so in semi-jest. I was once telling him of the different attitude towards youthful intemperance shown by two elderly Irishmen of the same generation and background, both brought up at Eton and at Cambridge. One of them, a Protestant, told me of how as a young man before 1914, he and a friend – who was afterwards killed in the Great War – went for a holiday in the Loire country. 'We drank Vouvray' he told me. 'And we didn't realise how strong it was. It was a very hot afternoon which made it worse. Of course, we weren't tight.' As if one would have held it against him, I thought, had he admitted that he and his friend got tight while on holiday in France half a century earlier. The other elderly Irishman, the Catholic writer Sir Shane Leslie, who sometimes stayed with Alfred at Fisher House, remembering a youthful trip to the Loire, said: 'I drank deep of the golden Vouvray wine and collapsed joyously into a ditch.' 'That's the Catholic attitude' said Alfred.

Sir Shane Leslie was one of a number of colourful and interesting people who came to stay with Alfred at Fisher House and whom I and other undergraduates had the good fortune to meet. Another was William De Geijer who had also been up at Cambridge before 1914 and had hunted with the Trinity Foot Beagles. He told me how, after hunting, he would have a partridge and a pint of champagne brought to his rooms with which he would refresh himself while the College servant was getting his bath ready. 'The highest pitch of human felicity' was Alfred's comment when I recounted this to him many years later.

Alfred was himself a keen follower of the Trinity Foot Beagles, during his years as Chaplain and afterwards; having been a foxhunter in his youth. Dressed with his customary elegance in breeches, black coat, stock and cloth cap, he enlivened most meets with his presence; he would give a party every year for the beaglers and also for those who followed the University Draghounds and the local hunt. He regarded himself as a beagler rather than a foxhunter, much as he had enjoyed foxhunting; and when speaking of foxhunting he would say that he had never had any ambition to hunt in the Shires, being content with the less fashionable foxhunting world of Essex and elsewhere.

It was all part of his innate modesty and contentment with his station in life. He never aspired to move in high society; a few friends round the fire was what he liked. Despite his remark about a partridge and a pint of champagne after beagling being the highest pitch of human felicity, champagne was not his favourite drink; he much preferred claret. He loved Cambridge because it was, in his opinion, homely, relaxed and unambitious. 'Oxford never takes its eye off London' he once said to me. 'Cambridge doesn't know that London exists.' A slight exaggeration, perhaps, at any rate as far as he, personally, was concerned; for in his tall hat and frock coat he was a not unfamiliar figure on the London train, on his way to or from some engagement in the metropolis.

Loving Cambridge as he did, the blow of having to leave it in 1965 after having lived there as Chaplain for thirty-three years would have been well nigh insupportable had it not been for his religious faith and his ability to make the best of what life held in store for him. His departure was almost as great a blow for the members of his flock, past and present; for most of them he *was* Cambridge; it was hard to imagine Cambridge and the Chaplaincy without him. At the time when he ceased to be Chaplain he was only sixty-four and in excellent health; one expected him to be there for at least another ten years. While there had been a growing opinion in certain quarters of the University that he was unsuited to be Chaplain to the type of young men who were now coming up to Cambridge in increasing numbers – it was even suggested that some of them might be intimidated by the sight of that essential work of reference, *Burke's Peerage*, on his bookshelves – the immediate cause of his departure was his refusal to admit women undergraduates to the Chaplaincy, where he wished to maintain the quasimonastic atmosphere that was then still to be found in the men's colleges; the women undergraduates having up to that time had a separate Chaplaincy of their own.

This gave rise to the myth that Alfred Gilbey disliked women, which could not have been further from the truth. He welcomed women to Fisher House as guests and numbered many women among his dearest friends. Whenever I met him he would ask: 'How's your dear mother?' and after I was married, 'How's your dear wife?' He had been devoted to his mother who was Spanish and deeply religious; it was through her that his branch of the Gilbeys became Catholic. His father had been obliged to become a Catholic in order to marry her; 'converted at pistol point' as Alfred put it when speaking to me of his parents; which more than ever confirms that he was not the avid 'maker of converts' which he is all too often represented as being. His parents' marriage was a great success and he got on well with his father, from whom he inherited, among other characteristics, his love of hunting. But while his father, after his conversion, had been a perfectly good Catholic, Alfred always maintained that he owed his religious faith to his mother; and he believed that another woman, his governess Miss Cairns, sowed the seeds of his vocation to the priesthood.

In *We Believe*, the book based on his course of instruction in the Catholic faith which a group of his friends persuaded him to publish some years after he had retired from the Chaplaincy, he speaks of sex as 'something sublime and sacred'. He had the highest possible regard for marriage and was always delighted to officiate at the weddings of former members of his flock and other friends. He officiated at my wedding and when signing the register made a point of talking to my staunchly Low Church Anglican father-in-law, who had been a Master of Foxhounds, about hunting. I am certain he did so as a way of cheering him up in case he was not feeling too happy after giving his only child in matrimony to a Catholic.

After retiring from the Chaplaincy, Alfred moved to London; living at first at the Athenaeum, one of his two clubs – the other being Buck's – then at the Travellers' Club, which he joined at about this time. He used to say that he felt entirely at home at the Travellers'; the Athenaeum having been above him intellectually and Buck's above him socially. What he said about Buck's he would certainly have said about Pratt's, which unexpectedly invited him to become an honorary member when he was in his eighties. He was greatly touched by this invitation and dining at Pratt's became one of the pleasures of his latter years.

Alfred lived at the Travellers' for almost the rest of his life. The club gave him a permanent bedroom and also a tiny room at the top of the back stairs which he made into an oratory. He would retire there to pray before the Blessed Sacrament, which Cardinal Heenan gave him a licence to reserve; and he would say Mass here once a week with a friend or two as his congregation. He used to say that it was like an oratory in Penal Times; in this respect it might have taken him back to his childhood for he also used to say that there was a flavour of Penal Times in the Sunday Masses in the private chapel at Mark Hall, the house in Essex where he grew up. His parents were allowed to have Mass in the house because the nearest Catholic church was eight miles away.

On other days of the week when he lived at the Travellers', Alfred said an early morning Mass at Brompton Oratory, where he had a small but faithful congregation. For many years he went there and back by bus; then his friend and confrère in the Order of Malta, the late Lord Craigmyle, put a car and driver at his disposal to take him to and from his morning Mass. Once a month he said Mass in the Jesuit house in Mount Street for people who had been members of his flock at Cambridge; it was always very well attended.

Alfred's masses attracted not only his friends but also people who did not know him but were devotees of the Tridentine or Old Rite. He never used any rite but the Tridentine, having been given permission to continue using it by Cardinal Heenan after the liturgical changes of Vatican II. While he was devoted to the Old Rite, he would say that if at some future date the Church authorities saw fit to withdraw this permission and he was obliged to say Mass in the New Rite, he would accept the situation unquestioningly. Obedience to his superiors in the Church was to Alfred a quintessential part of his priesthood.

During the thirty-three years when Alfred lived in London – as long a period as his years at the Cambridge Chaplaincy – he acted as spiritual adviser to a great many people. When one saw him sitting with somebody in the Travellers', he might have been just chatting to a friend; on the other hand he might have been instructing a convert or giving spiritual advice. He was also active in the Order of Malta which he had joined as a Chaplain in 1947; he rose to be Chaplain Conventual Grand Cross *ad honorem* in 1982. As well as his spiritual life Alfred had his friends, who were always coming to see him at the Travellers'; where they were welcomed as warmly and entertained as generously as they had been at Fisher House. And while many of them were former members of his flock, there were others whom he had got to know after he retired from the Chaplaincy; one could say that after leaving Cambridge he still had his flock and it continued to grow.

His spiritual work took him all over Britain and to the Continent; he went to officiate at weddings, baptisms, funerals and requiem Masses. When he was well into his nineties he went to the United States to help with the publicity of the American edition of *We Believe*. Some of his friends, myself included, tried to prevent him from going, fearing that the long flight might have proved fatal to someone of his age; but he went and returned none the worse for it, saying that what he had enjoyed most was lunching on Wall Street.

Alfred was frequently absent from London just for pleasure. In September, the Trinity Foot Beagles hunt in Northumberland; and until he was well into his nineties Alfred would go to Northumberland every September to hunt with them. Another annual event was a trip with Father Michael Napier to visit country houses. Architecture and in particular country house architecture was one of Alfred's interests. Though he naturally appreciated being invited as a guest to a country house, he was equally happy to visit country houses as a tourist, having no particular ambition to get to know their owners. Michael Napier shared his love of architecture and had an equally great knowledge of it. He was a friend and contemporary of mine at Cambridge where for almost the whole of our three years he was a devout Anglo-Catholic. Then, during our last term, I found him, to my great surprise, at Fisher House, being instructed by Alfred. 'It was not really very satisfactory' was all he said when I expressed my surprise at his defection from Anglicanism. Later he became a Father of the London Oratory, eventually becoming Superior.

At weekends, if he was not going somewhere else, Alfred went to Rose Hill, a house near Henley-on-Thames belonging to his cousin Walter Gilbey, who gave him a permanent bedroom here as well as a chapel and a library, where he kept most of the books which he used to have at Fisher House. He was able to have friends to stay at Rose Hill; once, when travelling back to London with him on the train after staying with him here, I witnessed an example of his cheerful resignation to the Will of God and also of the good luck with which he was usually blessed when travelling. He always travelled with his chalice, carrying it in a small case; it was one of his most treasured possessions, having been given to him by his parents when he was ordained; the precious stones from his mother's engagement ring had been set in its base after her death. When the train pulled out of the station where we had boarded it, Alfred suddenly remembered that he had left his chalice on the platform. He remained serene and calm; said that if it were God's Will that he should lose his chalice he would offer it up; but if he managed to get it back he would be most grateful. At the first stop he managed to speak through the window of our carriage to the station master, who said he would telephone the station where the chalice had been left to see if it could be found. At the second stop the station master came to our window to say that the chalice had been found and would be put on the next train to London. Alfred duly retrieved it at Paddington.

Some of Alfred's journeys from London were to stay with friends. He stayed with me and my family both in Ireland and in Suffolk. His first visit to me in Ireland was in 1968; he was accompanied by his young friend David Watkin, a convert like Michael Napier and an even greater expert on architecture; destined to become a distinguished architectural historian and Cambridge don. I took Alfred and David to see Lyons, a fine Georgian country house in County Kildare containing some wonderful rooms with frescoes. It then belonged to University College, Dublin. Alfred never had any compunction about invading buildings not in private occupation; he used to say that by walking boldly in one was usually able to see all one wanted to see of the building before one was apprehended and ejected. He also used to say that, as a hunting man, he found it rather fun to be in the position of the hare or the fox and to be chased. The hall door of Lyons was open and we went in; but no chase ensued, for the house appeared to be deserted. I was able to show my companions all that they wished to see, except for one of the frescoed rooms which was locked. Before we left, Alfred wished to visit the lavatory. We found one, but it had 'Ladies' written on the door. 'I can't go in the Ladies' Alfred protested; but David and I said of course he could, there wasn't a lady in the house. So he reluctantly went in. One had to pass through an ante-room before reaching the lavatory itself and while in this ante-room Alfred kept saying jocularly: 'There's a lady in here! There's a lady in here!' Suddenly his tone changed to abject apology and an embarrassed-looking girl emerged. She had been in there all the time without our knowing it. She hurried out of the house and then, as though heaping coals of fire, returned after a few moments with the key of the locked frescoed room so that we were able to see it after all.

The other memorable episode of that visit was during a dinner party which we gave for Alfred. It was at the time of the controversy over the Church's attitude to birth control. A lady sitting next to him at dinner said brightly: 'Do tell me, Monsignor, what do you think of the Pill?' 'I don't' was his reply.

Alfred used to say, when he was in his eighties, that this was the happiest time of his life; he would certainly have said the same until well into his nineties. He kept all his faculties until then and his health remained remarkably good; he attributed this to his going about as much as possible on foot. The only sign of his great age was that he became very bent. In his early nineties he had a new interest, the compiling of a book of his favourite passages from a wide selection of writers. It was published in 1993, ten years after *We Believe* first appeared, and was called *The Commonplace Book of Monsignor A. N. Gilbey*. He told me that he would have liked to have called it *Keeping the Jungle at Bay* but that the publishers would not agree to this.

In 1996, when he was ninety-five, Alfred suffered a grievous blow in the premature death of his friend Michael Napier. However, he remained serene and appeared in very good form when, in the following May, he came to Lourdes with the annual pilgrimage of the Order of Malta; except that he was now not so good at walking so had to be pushed about in a wheelchair. He had always loved Lourdes but had not been for some years and he told me and others that he had decided to come this year because it would be his last chance; he did not think he had much longer to live. That autumn he suffered another blow when the Travellers' Club decided he was too frail to live there any longer. He moved to a convent in West Kensington, where I visited him in the early spring of 1998, less than a month before he died. I found him in good heart; clearly the nuns were looking after him well. His room was spacious and had an air of Fisher House: plenty of books and, on the table, a decanter of sherry which he offered to me and my daughter and a friend who were with me. It was the day of the Countryside March, what I and many others prefer to think of as the Hunting March. We had taken part in it and so had the ninety-six-year-old Alfred.

Ronald Creighton-Jobe

It is almost impossible to separate Alfred Gilbey the man and Alfred Gilbey the priest since in him grace and nature were linked in such a singular fashion. He was an example of the truth that was central to his understanding of man's relationship with Almighty God. Each person is uniquely created to be the object and expression of God's superabundant love, which, in turn, is to be reflected in his relations with his fellow creatures. It is a love that is unmerited and without reserve, a pure miracle of grace. This vision was at the heart of Alfred's conception of the priesthood. It is the highest gift that God can bestow; to stand at the altar, to offer with the Divine Son the eternal sacrifice of Calvary, to insert himself, and the faithful for whom he is mediator with Christ, into the mystery of the life of the Trinity. Alfred's share in this priesthood never ceased to fill him with wonder and a profound sense of humility.

He was blessed, of course, with a loving family and happy childhood, which combined the security of a prosperous Edwardian mercantile background on his father's side with a warmth and deep piety from his Andalusian mother. His father had become a Catholic to marry Maria Victorina de Ysasi of Jerez de la Frontera, and, although his instruction in the faith was somewhat rudimentary, he brought up his large Catholic family in an exemplary manner and the private chapel with daily Mass and the presence of the Blessed Sacrament was at the heart of family life at Mark Hall. From his mother and his beloved Spanish nurse he learned his prayers, the simple prayers which were to remain the bedrock of his spiritual life to the day he died. Alfred always maintained that his was an uncomplicated faith and in a sense it was true. He never doubted God's providence, and even when a sister died young of a brain tumour after a harrowing visit to Lourdes, the realisation that whatever happens to us is either willed by God or allowed by God for a purpose informed his vision of this life as but a preparation for the life of the world to come. His was a practical faith based on absolute acceptance of the supernatural as revealed by God to His Church through the guarantees of the Holy Spirit.

His Jesuit education at Beaumont was central to Alfred's spiritual formation. It is often said that the life in such an institution either makes a boy's faith or destroys it. This is both harsh and untrue, but in Gilbey's faith the simple meditations based on the methods of St Ignatius were central, and their influence enduring. He was not at home or at ease with Carmelite tradition, though he admired it greatly. He loved the classic expression of Benedictine life, with its ordered rhythm of prayer, work and study, and the beauty of the public worship of the sacred liturgy, but a child of the Society of Jesus he remained. Of the many changes in its life after the Second Vatican Council and the closure of Beaumont he could hardly bring himself to speak, so painful he found them. Characteristically his silence was an expression of his constant striving for charity. With his passionate Spanish nature, inherited from his mother, this was never easy and God alone knows how much this interior struggle must have cost him.

As should be the case with all priests, the Mass was at the centre of Alfred Gilbey's priestly life. He used to say that, ultimately, a priest's vocation was not to give himself to the faithful, but to give them God, most especially when, as an 'alter Christus', he stands at the altar joining in the self-offering of the Son of God to His eternal Father on our behalf. For over thirty years in London, with the exception of his first Thursday or Friday Masses in the Sodality Chapel at Farm Street, he celebrated the traditional rite in St Wilfrid's Chapel in the London Oratory, which became his spiritual home, and an important centre for his apostolate. It was here that he said his last Mass on the Feast of the Annunciation, so suitable a feast for Alfred, who never tired of praising the miracle of the Word made flesh, who in the Mass continues to dwell amongst us. Someone described one of those Masses celebrated in his extreme old age:

For me the most unforgettable thing about the unforgettable Mgr Gilbey was the moment when, before Communion, he turned from the altar and with his left hand lovingly holding the chalice, cupped beneath his right, tenderly and with a certain shyness confided to his congregation: 'Ecce Agnus Dei, ecce qui tollit peccata mundi.' The gesture and the attitude could not have been less triumphalist, or less distracted, the two failings one notices most frequently at that point in the Mass. Mgr Gilbey did not raise the Host, and he certainly did not look at the congregation. He remained slightly hunched over it – hunched AROUND it might be a more accurate description, embracing it from a distance. The facial expression was that of a grandfather holding his first grandchild for the first time. Never did body-language speak more unmistakably of loving protection, tinged with extreme pride in the protected one. This was something enormous, so enormous that he hardly dared whisper it to us; but it was not the enormity of an all-powerful God, even an all-powerful God who emptied Himself and took on the form of something less than a slave; rather it was the enormity of the tiny miracle that is a newborn baby. Until that moment the priest and his vulnerable God had been safe together at the altar, isolated together in their joint miracle; now they have to face the world and admit to it the extraordinary thing that has happened.

Before such a mystery man can only bow in adoration and thanksgiving and praise.

Much has been made of Gilbey's devotion to the old rite of Mass. True, like Father Faber, he saw it as the 'most beautiful thing this side of heaven' and found the vernacular translation of the novus order unbearably banal, but it was its unworthiness of the setting of sacred mystery unfolding in the Mass that so much distressed him. He rejoiced in the London Oratory's maintenance of a continuity in the Latin rite, and when the indult for the wider availability of the Tridentine Mass was granted in response to the Lefèbvrist crisis, Alfred was extremely cautious in welcoming it. He remained puzzled at the thought of a variety of 'Roman rites'. This attitude pained some traditionalists (a term he disliked), but his emphasis on the need for obedience to the Church and charity towards others made him unwilling to enter the world of ecclesiastical politics. In the end, he was deeply moved by the witness of many young priests, ordained since the upheavals of the Second Vatican Council, who were drawn to a deep love of Christ through celebrating the traditional rite of Mass. But discord and disharmony he could not abide, and he saw it as another attempt on the part of the devil to draw fallen human creatures into his own disorder and despair.

One of the other functions in a priest's life is to teach. Alfred always maintained that he was not an intellectual, and in this his innate modesty did not do credit to his real gifts as a communicator of the great truths of the faith. He was not an innovative thinker and indeed he would have shrunk from the very term; but his solid Jesuit grounding in clear, philosophical principles, and the years at the Beda College in Rome, preparing for the priesthood, enabled him to instruct generations of converts both at Cambridge, and later in London, with consummate skill and clarity. As is well known, he was loath to put pen to paper, but his instructions, transcribed and edited, made his book *We Believe* a masterpiece of its kind and, rather unexpectedly, given the climate of the post-conciliar Church, an enduring best seller. But perhaps it was precisely because of the collapse of sound catechetical principles in so many quarters that the book was such a resounding success. He would go anywhere and see anyone to promote it, not out of any sense of self-advertisement, but out of a burning desire to save souls. This led him as far afield as the United States, where, in a coast to coast tour, which would have daunted many a younger man, he enchanted American audiences. The sight of the nonagenarian Monsignor and the redoubtable Mother Angelica together on the television must rank as one of the most remarkable events in religious broadcasting for a very long time. He returned exhausted but deeply satisfied – and amused – by the whole experience.

In 1993 *The Commonplace Book of Monsignor A. N. Gilbey* was published containing passages from a collection of his favourite books. In it he states firmly: 'No one should take this book too seriously. Anyone who wants to know what I think seriously about almost every subject has only to turn to *We Believe* 'by a Priest'. In fact, the *Commonplace Book* is far from frivolous, with many of the selections challenging the accepted orthodoxy of the modern world and its misguided egalitarianism. But it is true that *We Believe* is, in concrete terms, Alfred's abiding memorial as the priest fulfilling his role as teacher of the faithful.

Gilbey never tired of saying how grateful to God he was for calling him to the secular priesthood. Devoted as he was to the old Society of Jesus before the upheavals of the 1960s, it never seriously occurred to him to try his vocation as a Jesuit. He admired their discipline, practicality and integrity, but that particular calling to serve God was not for him. The monastic life, with its ordered rhythm of prayer and its devotion to the liturgy, appealed to his romantic and aesthetic side, and his association with the Benedictine public schools remained close, particularly through the many undergraduates who came up to Cambridge from them. But Alfred's many gifts did not include the ability to carry a tune, and his closest monastic friends were those who did not necessarily find fulfilment in the stability of the cloister.

The post-Tridentine reforms brought many blessings to the Church, but Alfred often observed that one of the more unhelpful developments which accompanied their implementations was a tendency to turn secular priests into quasi-religious. The vowed life of poverty, chastity and obedience is a very particular vocation and one of the dangers in converting seminaries into institutions which resembled monasteries was to give the impression that the secular priesthood was somehow a second best in comparison. This Gilbey deplored. Much has been made of his being ordained on his 'own patrimony', an option no longer possible in the new code of canon law. By paying for his own education a man ordained to the priesthood enjoyed a certain degree of independence in his relations with his bishop. But Alfred championed an understanding of the secular priest's role which owed more to the medieval system than to the post-Tridentine period. It was this that gave him a certain sympathy for the remnants of this sacerdotal autonomy in the canonical structures of the Church of England. He was to live to see the vestiges of this being swept away in that institution, as well as some of the attractive social survivals which had endeared to him the externals of the world of Barchester. His Spanish dimension deplored the over-centralisation of the Roman dicasteries which produced clerical bureaucrats devoid of any real sense of the Church's more profound theological understanding of tradition. He was immensely gratified when he was elected to the Old Brotherhood, a select group of the secular clergy. He felt it as a seal of approval for a priest who did not always conform to the conventional idea of a Catholic cleric. He loved the Oratory of St Philip because of its unique combination of collegiate life, dedication to prayer and liturgical splendour, and the ordinary life of a secular priest, with its inner rhythms formed by the administration of the sacraments, preaching and pastoral labours. His own exercise of spiritual fatherhood, infectious gaiety and his gift for deep and enduring friendships had much in common with that holy Florentine turned Roman.

In the end the inner life of any priest remains hidden, known only to God. Although deeply affectionate, even passionate by nature, Alfred Gilbey was immensely reserved about himself. He gave himself unstintingly, indeed his own brand of asceticism was to be always available to those who sought him, no matter how demanding they might be. How much this cost him, God alone knows. How painful it was for him to see the destruction of so much of civilised Christian life one can only just begin to imagine. But he remained rigorously detached – not indifferent. Day after day, year after year, his routine of Mass, rosary and visits to the Blessed Sacrament sustained him. The sanctuary lamp in his tiny chapel in the Travellers' Club was a beacon and an anchor. But he, too, was a rock of refuge and sign of hope to untold numbers of his spiritual children who found in Alfred the priest a father and friend *par excellence*.

Charles des Forges

As a child I was enchanted by the story of the Wisdom of Solomon and his device for discovering the true mother of the disputed baby. I decided that I should like to be wise. 'Truth alone is worthy of our entire devotion' is the prefatory quotation to *We Believe*. To be wise one must know and live the truth. Monsignor Gilbey's central motivation was the need to adhere to the truth. In meeting him I met the wise man who could help me to wisdom.

In 1965 my father was sitting in Warwick Street church waiting for Mass when a pious lady in front of him asked of him to be the altar server. The priest was already on his way from the sacristy to the altar. My father stopped him and said, 'I have been invited to serve your Mass.' The priest looked and nodded. My father added: 'I'm afraid I don't speak any English.' With a twinkle in his eye, the priest replied, 'Oh good! Neither do I.' The priest was Monsignor Gilbey, and my father and he were firm friends thereafter. My friendship with the Monsignor followed my father's.

Monsignor Gilbey gave hospitality and counsel most generously. He inspired in his young friends a combined sense of awe and intimacy; one somehow felt he was allowing one to share his life. The gift of a rosary, being allowed to sew buttons on his cassock, sitting talking with him in his room, such things contributed to an easy friendship. The generation difference became an enhancement and not in any way a handicap.

On 2 November 1994, my twenty-first birthday, Monsignor Gilbey gave me a copy of 'one of two books I never wrote', *We Believe*, the transcription of Monsignor Gilbey's course of instruction to those interested in the faith. From the first page, I could not put the book down. I was not an enquirer but a cradle Catholic, educated at Catholic schools, but Monsignor Gilbey's exposition was a revelation to me. I was thrilled at discovering all these things that I believed but that I never knew I believed. Whereas for many their focus concerning Monsignor Gilbey has been his person, for me, with all the warmth that developed between us, it has always been his marvellous exposition of the faith. On the frequent occasions I came to be his guest at the Travellers' Club I would keenly look forward to talking with him about some part of his book. Of it he said, in the prologue to his *Commonplace* book, 'Anyone who wants to know what I think seriously about almost every subject has only to read *We Believe* "by a Priest".'

I have often been told that *We Believe* is a pre-Vatican II course and that things don't work that way anymore. Yet however deeply I have searched elsewhere, be it the Saints, the Catechism, the Holy Father's encyclicals or the documents of the Second Vatican Council, when I have returned I have always found that it remains in perfect harmony with all these sources. When someone has presented a piece of doctrine which was unfamiliar to me I have been able to hold it against the model of *We Believe* to know whether it was Catholic or not.

Monsignor Gilbey always marvelled that a young man such as myself, educated at an eminent Catholic public school, did not know what Hope was or what Grace performed. There is now a thirst among young Catholics to know their faith better. Herein may lie a posthumous mission for Monsignor Gilbey through his book. In a world which is shy of giving to the young too much catechesis lest, supposedly, they be frightened away – often putting in its place a woolly and subjective approach – I have found that they have been reassured by the thoroughness and precision of Monsignor Gilbey's exposition. The book exudes his confidence in the truth of our faith such that it is infectious. So coherent and so straightforward is the presentation that whenever I give it to a friend I always warn him or her not to be tempted to go and argue it out with others; Monsignor Gilbey never did this, he simply stated the truth to those who wanted to hear it. Instead of arguing in a sea of opinions, the young can once again proclaim what they believe.

The story of my father's first meeting with Monsignor Gilbey might seem to give comfort to an idea of Monsignor Gilbey as someone constantly railing against the Second Vatican Council. In all my time spent with Monsignor Gilbey, I cannot recall him once being critical of it. 'The here and now is the only time I have in which, with God's grace, to work out my salvation. In that task the ideal Church, whether of the past or of the future, is powerless to help me.' (*We Believe*, chapter 8.) He often quoted to me the passage from John 15 about the vine and the branches and said that if a man separate himself from the Church then he has cut himself off from the source of life. He loved to show me the hand-written card from Cardinal Heenan that read: 'You should have no hesitation in celebrating the Tridentine Mass either in private or in public' – for which he used the version as surviving in 1955. He assured me that this was the only reason that he would say the old Mass. It had been given as special permission because he was beyond retirement age at the time of the suppression of the Old Rite. Because of this his Masses had none of the rebellious atmosphere of other Tridentine Masses I have attended, where talk is constantly lurking of the universal restoration of the Old Rite. What was so lovely about the old Mass with Monsignor Gilbey was that it was unselfconscious. One just went to Mass and then got on with the rest of one's day.

What most brought us together was his traditional Catholic piety. I marvelled that whereas many seemed to think that devotion to Our Lady is unfashionable and embarrassing, he knew not only that it is not an optional extra but is essential to the Catholic faith. It seems to me that devotion to Our Lady is like a step of faith from within the faith. It has to be taken for one to appreciate its truth. It was Monsignor's great devotion that drove me to keep trying to embrace the motherhood of Mary amidst the barracking of my evangelical Protestant friends. It is the sweetest victory to be won. I love to remember Monsignor Gilbey sitting in his big leather chair in his bedroom at the Travellers', head bowed, eyes closed and slowly feeling his rosary beads through his fingers.

In 1997 I served at his Mass on the Feast of the Assumption of the Blessed Virgin, which is his ordination day. This was to be his last Mass in which he would celebrate this anniversary on earth. In the silence of Tenterden parish church there was only one other friend present. At the consecration I beheld a specially tender love for Our Lord in the Blessed Sacrament that filled his face and his eyes.

Towards the end of January 1998 it was decided that Monsignor Gilbey should move on from his permanent bedroom at the Travellers'. I was asked to stay at the Club in the time that remained until the move to give any assistance that I might. It was a busy three weeks for the many friends who came to help him. Amidst all the hustle Monsignor Gilbey serenely continued his daily rhythm. I remember sitting in a taxi going to Nazareth House where a room had suddenly become available. Time was running on, and we had only seen one painfully cramped nursing home and Westminster Cathedral could offer no solution. I looked up at his face. His expression was like that of a child that is being shielded from the gravity of the situation and is playing along, though it is quite aware really of what is going on. It summed up for me complete trust in the benevolent Fatherhood of God.

A little after seven o'clock on his penultimate evening in the Travellers', I arrived in his bedroom in order to escort him down to dinner. He was sitting in his leather armchair saying his rosary. He looked up and smiled, but the smile broke into being a 'brave face'. Thirty-eight years in his home were coming to an end. For the first time I saw how distressing the change was for him. There was nothing I could say or wanted to say. I crossed the room and sat on the floor, resting my head on the arm of the chair. We sat in silence for a quarter of an hour, I looking up now and again to see his face. Finally he bid that we go downstairs. I asked if we could say a decade together – which we did – and then for his blessing. He laid his hand upon my head and I closed my eyes while he silently blessed me. That is how I like to remember being with Monsignor Gilbey.

The last couple of days passed swiftly. The move was conducted efficiently. We stripped the walls of the pictures of the places he loved so much – Mark Hall, Beaumont, Cambridge and Rome; we bundled the many unopened envelopes into boxes. I was particularly delighted to find among his belongings a discipline and a spiky belt. One isn't used to seeing these marvellous old forms of penance, and it appealed to my admiration for the ascetical tradition. When we arrived at Nazareth House, the Irish nun in charge, Sister Brenda, said with wonderful simplicity, 'He's come here to die.' I thought how little she knew Monsignor Gilbey.

I was out of the country and uncontactable for the next two months. I telephoned my mother on Easter Saturday and she told me that Monsignor Gilbey had died on 26 March and that his funeral had been conducted at the Brompton Oratory. My thoughts raced back to that time – remembering that I had prayed for him specially one day – and it had been that day. Yet I have been still more delighted. The whole of his catechesis had centred on the Incarnation, and that all other mysteries were either leading up to it or a consequence of it. He was taken ill before he could say his Mass on the 26th, so the last Mass he celebrated was on the Feast of the Annunciation – the Incarnation. Praise the Lord!

I have never felt anything of a separation. He could well be in the Travellers' now. I pray to him often and have felt most keenly his intercession, particularly in finding the monastic order of the Community of St John with its charisma to search for truth at all levels.

I often think of his arrival in Heaven, and how Our Blessed Lord may have greeted him at His throne: 'Who made you?' – 'God made me.' 'Why did God make you?' – 'To know Him, love Him and serve Him in this world ... [*long pause*] ... and to be happy with Him forever in the next ...'

Jack Gold

MARK HALL

Mark Hall, Harlow, was approached by a long drive from a point opposite the lane to the Essex Hunt kennels. The flat park divided into paddocks, with three gateways between the Lodge on the old coach road to London, and the house and Parndon church. The stables and large kitchen garden were nearby to the east, and the pleasure garden sloped downhill to the river and railway line some half a mile away. The whole area is now transformed by the construction of the large satellite town of Harlow New Town and the destruction by fire which totally destroyed the house. There is now nothing to indicate the site of the house except a street name, Parndon church and its graveyard with its Gilbey family tombs alone surviving.

In its final form Mark Hall was fronted by a long symmetrical nine-windowed elevation, with two bays and a portico, in late eighteenth-century style. It was probably built in 1819 by Richard Arkwright, son of the inventor of the spinning frame, when the estate was bought for one of his own five sons, at a time when the classical style was losing its severity. The pediments over the windows foreshadow the decline of the Adam style, and the comparatively low ceilings for a house of its size suggest that the east front was an addition to a more modest house, following the height of the earlier rooms.

The other reception rooms seemed more late Victorian in appearance, largely due to their fashionable upholstery, some of which may have come from the large London home in Westbourne Terrace. (It is notable that all the Berkshire Gilbeys had set up house near Paddington Station, while the Essex partners – Golds,

Gilbeys, Blyths – had houses near their Oxford Street office, eventually concentrating on Portland Place and Regent's Park.) The draped red and brown velvet curtains seemed very out of date by the 1920s when the writer first saw them.

Upstairs the bedrooms facing the park must have been very peasant, but as a youthful bachelor I was relegated to the former nursery, now the bachelors' wing which had been added much later to accommodate the sons of the house, interspersed with some housemaids' cupboards. Bathrooms were few and there were pantries, lamp room and other offices below. An unusual feature of a household supplied by a butler with two footmen and unlimited housemaids was that the sons of the house all cleaned their own very elegant shoes, whether by choice or decree I never discovered.

Another domestic surprise was to hear Cousin Newman address his chauffeur as Gilbey. This was no slip of the tongue: that was indeed his name, and he was said to be a very distant cousin.

There were of course the usual numbers of grooms and gardeners customary for a large household and a splendid kitchen garden which included a row of earth closets then only recently superseded by the installation of some more convenient alternatives indoors.

After Newman Gilbey's death none of the family wanted to renew the lease, given the threat of Harlow New Town, and the owner, Loftus Arkwright, apparently thought another tenant unlikely; so the contents were put up for auction, including the mahogany sideboard and cupboards specially made to fit the alcoves of the dining room.

I attended the view day, when the usual crowd of inquisitive neighbours filled the house, but few of the family attended. An exception was Frank Gilbey, the third son, who was something of a connoisseur. He was also exceptionally handsome in a Spanish way, with manners to match his looks. I happened to witness his meeting with Loftus Arkwright, who arrived at the front door just as Frank was leaving. Frank's greeting of the owner of the house was so elegant and self-assured that any witness would have thought their roles were reversed.

I left bids for some of the dining room furniture and a few days later two handsome mahogany cupboards and a pair of black basalt vases were installed at Little Codham Hall and are now in our London house.

Mark Hall was later used as a hostel for Land Girls, who succeeded in burning it down so completely that it was a total loss and Harlow New Town has now obliterated the whole area.

Peter Gregory-Jones

ALFRED GILBEY: A PERSONAL SIGHTING

When I first saw Alfred Gilbey he was wreathed in the dappled light of a mid-seventies' summer sunset. He was in the company of two much younger men, somewhere in their mid-thirties, I supposed. One had short dark hair and wore small, round and challengingly unfashionable tortoiseshell spectacles; his silk gown was thrown over his left shoulder, and occasionally brushed the paving stones. The other had a roseate slightly tanned complexion and a beautifully cut mane of tawny blond hair which the breeze and the westering light caught at after each long slow stride. Both were tall and enviably debonair.

But it was the older, slighter figure who walked between them who had most secured my attention, as this elegant and self-contained trio sauntered along King's Parade, in the direction of St Botolph's and the University Press. The echoes of their quiet laughter vanished at the same moment as the street lamps suddenly stuttered into horrid neon light. Dressed in a closely-fitting clerical frock-coat and a priest of priest's round black hat, he angled his tightly-furled umbrella more in the manner of an *ancien régime* cane than as an actual aid to walking. It was an engaging and intriguing scene. At the same time, there was nothing theatrical about its central character. The entire mien of this elderly priest spoke to me of well-appointed libraries and secluded chapels. So who was he, I asked myself with happy curiosity as I turned my bicycle round and rode back down Bene't Street? He had to be Anglican, of that I was sure. No Roman priest of my acquaintance was so poised. The aura that he left behind was redolent of a quieter Chancellor Garth Moore,[a] a less rickety

[a] The Worshipful Chancellor, the Rev. Evelyn Garth Moore (1906–90). Barrister-at-law, Fellow of Corpus Christi College, Cambridge, Chancellor of the Diocese of

and unpredictable Canon Simpson of Trinity, and an altogether more seemly version of the Rev Dr Cuthbert Cupitt Keet, the aged incumbent of St Clement's in Bridge Street and my own parish priest at that time. Moreover, I told myself that this demure yet electrifying figure was no Anglo-Catholic. Too smart and too relaxed to be part of that often overwrought and somewhat tatty ambience.

No: he could only be an old-fashioned and dry Anglican[b] – blue copes and ante-communion; a Dean of Chapel possibly, a Reader at the Divinity School: a Trollopian figure in any case, and not a latter-day emanation of Pusey or Hurrell Froude. Whatever else, here was no emissary from Rome!

The following morning, which was a Sunday and one that summer's sweetest, I took myself off to Little St Mary's, knowing that the vicar, Fr James Owen, was better acquainted with the university and its denizens than the unworldly Dr Keet. After Mass, I reported my sighting to him as we walked round to his house in Newnham Terrace.

'That "vision of a quintessentially happier Cambridge, now all but lost" as you so lyrically put it, was, sir, none other than the Right Reverend Monsignor Alfred Newman Gilbey, former Roman Catholic Chaplain here. I was Chaplain at Jesus at the time of his sudden departure. December 1965. All very untoward; practically forced to leave, you see.'

'"Roman Catholic? ... Forced to leave? ..."' – I interrupted the sonorous flow.

'Peter, do sit down again for goodness sake. Drink your sherry and eat up that Bath Oliver. Excellent. Now, as I was trying to tell you.'

He proceeded with his own highly partial but desperately loyal version of the events leading up to and surrounding Mgr Gilbey's

---

Durham (1954–89). His blood-curdling sermons at St Clement's, Cambridge on the Feast of King Charles Martyr struck a Savonarolian note amidst those otherwise rather musty ceremonials.

[b] Years later, echoing the gentle strictures of Winstanley, his old history tutor at Trinity, Alfred told me that had he been born Anglican, he would have been 'a High and not an Anglo'.

resignation, accompanied by thumbnail sketches and dazzling imi-
tations of those involved – the most withering being reserved for
Mgr Gilbey's immediate successor, Fr Richard Incledon, and the
latter's King Charles spaniel.

'That dog, my dear, was positively Cromwellian. Barely a term
into the new régime and man's best friend was prancing and
snuffling about the rubble that had once been a perfectly decent
baldacchino, from the old Upper Chapel, you know.'

I didn't, but soon was to. It had been a brilliant performance.
With a final yap, he slumped back into his chair. He grinned
broadly, but his eyes remained sad and troubled as they had been
throughout this *tour de force*.

Presently it was time for us to part, so I drained my glass and we
said our goodbyes. I left with a heavy heart. For while my initial
curiosity had been well and truly satisfied,[c] the images which Fr
Owen had conjured up, apparently so playfully, had already firmly
impressed themselves. They seemed hardly credible – sweating
undergraduates wielding pickaxes in the afternoon sun as they
smashed down plaster pillars and ripped out panelling; or of an
unprotected grand piano[d] discovered one bleak winter's lunchtime
supporting a trestle table stacked with hammers and open paint
tins. Such seemingly mindless destruction of Church fabric and
property was of course not unknown elsewhere in the dreary wake
of the Second Vatican Council, but that it had also apparently happened here in Cambridge transformed what had previously been a
generalised aesthetic and intellectual disapprobation into something less cerebral and more personal. Ridiculously, no doubt, but
somehow or other I wished to make amends.

---

[c] I had also learnt the 'most probable' identity of Mgr Gilbey's two companions.
'The dark one will have been David Watkin, a Peterhouse don … the other Alastair
Langlands, I think an old Trinity Hall man, and an absolute charmer. All three
would have been dining together at Trinity.'
[d] The piano previously belonged to the sister of Outram Evennett (1901–64),
Fellow of Trinity and long-standing Secretary (1931–42) and then Chairman
(1942–64) of the Cambridge University Catholic Association; one of Mgr Gilbey's
closest friends and staunchest supporters.

Later that summer I had another similarly climacteric experience when I was taken to visit the Catholic church at Bury St Edmunds.

When seen from without, Charles Day's 1830s Greek Revival church at Bury, with its Ionic portico and generally unassuming and unflustered air, still sets off quiet echoes more redolent of Penal Times than the Wisemanian revival which was soon to embolden English Catholicism. The interior, however, has been desecrated. Stripped of its architecturally necessary furnishing, the church neither looks, sounds nor smells like a place of worship or devotion. It is lacking in anything vaguely approximating to the numinous. Newman might never have been. This was my first visit, and it was suddenly clear that something very akin had happened to the chapels at Fisher House, though here it was writ large, for all to see. Distraught and angry, I stomped out into the leaden late August afternoon.

It was because of this experience and partly on account of James Owen's revelations, but principally as a result of having seen that 'quintessential' silhouette, side-lit by a June sunset, that earlier and hazier intentions now crystallised into a single resolve. To meet Mgr Gilbey, and tell him that I wanted to try to write the history of the Cambridge Catholic Chaplaincy which, to my astonishment, I had learnt did not then exist.

Several months were to pass, however, before I took up the gauntlet I had thrown down for myself. Mainly because I had been settling into my first job, at the King's School, Rochester: that autumn, my time belonged to others.

But immediately after Christmas I wrote to Fr Owen asking him for Mgr Gilbey's address. However, before receiving his reply I overheard a (very noisy) conversation in my own club which supplied me with the information. It was a typically misogynous exchange between ageing clubmen who had lunched well, and it concluded more or less like this:

'Can't imagine how he did it.'

'How who did what?'

'Old Gilbey.'

'Ah! What though?'

'How he wangled it to live full time at the Travellers'.'

'No wife of course. Children?'

'I shouldn't think so.'

I preferred to believe that 'old Gilbey' had achieved his domiciliary status more by charm than guile. Be that as it may, I could now enact my plan.

Accordingly, one dank and freezing Sunday morning in early February 1976 I caught an empty train up to Charing Cross. Invaded by curious undulating layers of opalescent fog, Pall Mall was silent to the point of eeriness. Having neither written nor telephoned, when I arrived at the club's heavily-shut doors I was suddenly reminded of the Mole turning up unannounced at Mr Badger's snowy threshold. And although SW1 is hardly the Wild Wood, my misgivings almost got the worse of me. However, when I rang the bell and the door was eventually heaved open by a dishevelled porter with a Dublin accent and a Guinnessy belch, my anthropomorphic fantasising was (quite literally) blown back into the fog. I gave my name and asked whether Mgr Gilbey were in.

'Oh, to be sure he's in, he is. That is, if he didn't just go out. I'll be calling his likes for you. Now you just wait over there by the fire, even if it's not lit, today being a Sunday.'

This knockabout turn lasted all of five seconds while he ushered me to a chair in the hall, before lurching back to his little lobby.

I didn't have long to wait, which was as well because my earlier misgivings were resurfacing, before a familiar figure slipped into my range of vision, neatly circumvented an obtruding table and was, as it were, upon me. Being huddled in a heavy coat[e] and encumbered by hat, gloves and scarf, I only just managed to get to my feet in time.

An outstretched hand; a smile which was both quizzical and quixotic. Then the opening salvo: 'My dear boy, forgive me, I don't quite remember you and perhaps I didn't catch your name properly – Peter Gregory-Jones? The porters on Sundays are ... well.'

My first overriding impression of Alfred Gilbey at close hand

---

[e] On whose velvet collar Mgr Gilbey at once complimented me.

was not so much the man's poise and gravitas as his aura of cleanliness. A reassuring, masculine, nursery smell of Pear's soap, freshly-ironed linen, the careful use of starch: this much at least my nose seemed to inform me. His long hands were exquisite, Düreresque and beautifully cared for.[f] They were also radiantly clean. No Edwardian nanny, whether Spanish or Essex-born, could have demanded more from her former charge.

'So you still want to write the history of the Chaplaincy? As I said earlier, a most laudable aim. I think though that I ought to warn you that you and I will probably be your book's only readers.'

When Alfred[g] said this I was on the point of taking my leave and we were getting up from our chairs by the fire at the Oxford and Cambridge Club, where earlier he had given me a princely luncheon.[h]

It seemed a paradoxical warning, and rather nonplussed me. For Alfred had spent half a day reliving for my benefit remote dramas from his time as Chaplain, and recounting anecdotes with all the verve of a James Owen, yet with none of the latter's underlying bitterness or resentment. He had also suggested how and where I should start my researches. Indeed he had just handed me a letter of introduction to the Westminster Cathedral Archivist, Miss Powyser.

As Alfred's enthusiasm had grown for what he was already calling 'our joint project', so too had the feeling of intimacy between us. It was difficult to believe that we had met only hours before.

'Oh, I'm utterly certain, Father. I don't believe in destiny in any formal sense. But I do believe in Divine Providence. I can't really

---

[f] 'I am very fortunate', he once told me à propos the attention he paid to his hands, 'that my natural vanity is in this case partly justified by being a priest. Every day I hold Our Blessed Lord between these' – he held his hands out, as if for a prefectorial inspection.

[g] For the sake of convenience, from here onwards I shall use the simple appellative 'Alfred', even if several months were to pass before, at his bidding, I stopped calling him 'Monsignor' or 'Father'.

[h] Contrary to clubland mythology, which maintained that the best that the O. and C.'s kitchens could come up with was broiled mutton and kale, with turnips on Race Night, we had eaten that day superb sirloin of beef, accompanied by two bottles of superber claret, with Welsh rarebits to follow.

imagine why or how, but this "project" seems to have been ... sent me. I feel, well, entrusted with it.'

I also felt embarrassed at this self-important-sounding declaration. But Alfred smiled delightedly.

'My dear boy! And what fun we're going to have together. Ring me up soon and invite yourself to dinner. I say Mass at the Travellers' most Wednesday evenings at 6.30.'

With that he sat down again, drew a reading lamp on to his lap and opened his breviary. I tiptoed away across the Turkey carpet, retrieved my greatcoat and other wintry paraphernalia and walked out into the fog and silence. My heart was lighter now.

We had both had a more than agreeable and mutually profitable afternoon. I had seldom been so entertained or charmed nor, for that matter, so utterly flattered. It was flattery which had taken the form of encouragement: affectionate but dispassionate, wholehearted but also cool and even slightly wary – yet flattery all the same.

However, recalling now the warm tones and fleeting nuances of that short winter's day, I don't think the rippling success of our first meeting can be solely attributed to the fact that I desired to write the book which for long years Alfred had wanted to see written.

No, it was also a question of mutual attraction – not sexual, but aesthetic and, as far as I was concerned, social too. I was young, personable and full of enthusiasm; he was elderly, elegant and self-possessed: a classic recipe. Beauty might be relative; but gesture, tone of voice and accent, the ways a person moves, how he smiles and what his eyes tell you, are objective realities, which can be measured and assessed. In this respect, neither of us had apparently found the other wanting.

'Even as I speak I believe there are Guardian Angels hovering in this room. But I don't expect to see them.'[1]

The room was the dining room at Rose Hill, in Alfred's Cousin Walter's Edwardian country house high above the Thames Valley and not far from Henley. Lunch was long over, but we were still sitting round the table, sipping Gilbey's 'J' port and nibbling water biscuits as another winter's afternoon darkened into evening.

Andrew Wilson had come to interview Alfred for an article

which appeared shortly afterwards. As a result, the conversation had been more theological than anecdotal; less gay and confidential than usual, though arresting as ever. On that occasion Alfred presided as a Protonotary Apostolic of Holy Mother Church. It was an impressive performance and an illuminating experience.

At the mention of Guardian Angels, I caught not only myself but also Andrew Wilson, in his most reputable 'Young Fogey' suit,[i] casting a fleeting upward glance. That we were both captivated by the notion was evident; an *ex cathedra* reiteration, as it were, of the lulling bedside chatter of Christian mothers and nannies down the generations.[j] We were perhaps also slightly incredulous.

But when Alfred, after delivering himself of this neglected Eternal Truth, leant back in his chair, and the fading light transformed him into an almost inquisitorial figure,[k] there was no longer any room for doubt that what he had avowed he had meant quite literally. This affirmation was no exercise of religious whimsy designed to charm those whose doctrinal development had been arrested in the nursery. Rather, it revealed the religious humility, which in turn rested upon a bedrock faith, of an otherwise subtle and sophisticated, yet disciplined and logical mind; a mind that above all else sought and responded to revealed truth. This had certainly been Alfred at his most enchanting, but also at his most categorical.

Not until his very last years, when dressing became an almost insurmountable effort, did Alfred wear a cassock in the public rooms at the Travellers' (or in any other of the clubs to which he belonged). The one exception was at lunchtime in highest summer,

---

[i] 'Young Fogeyism', a socio-journalistic phenomenon – forgotten now? – which was reaching its apogee in those years. See *The Young Fogey Handbook, or A Guide to Backwards Mobility*, edited by Suzanne Lowry, 1985. Alfred as a YF, i.e. a neo-conservative, hero appears on p.34.

[j] 'May Angels guard you while you sleep and bring you sweet repose; and grant you safety now until morning light appears. God bless and love you, my darling.' I once murmured this prayer to Alfred, who was down with a heavy cold, as I tucked him up for the night at the Travellers', and moved him to gentle, nostalgic tears. The next morning he got me to write the prayer down, urging me as I did so to 'make very sure you say that to your boy every night when you put *him* to bed; so incredibly important, you know.'

[k] The photographer, John Timbers, caught this moment perfectly.

when he would take his favourite table at the near end of the Coffee Room, wearing 'what, my dear, I call my Oratorian day-dress' – consciously echoing a Lopesian[l] turn of phrase.

Alfred's reluctance to wear a cassock under such circumstances was not, I think, solely or even principally dictated by a desire not to arouse any anti-Popish sentiments which some of his fellow members might have harboured. It was a question of coherence and personal taste. He had reached sartorial maturity in the early 1920s, when gentlemanly English Catholic priests wore clerical frock-coats and black silk waistcoats. Soutanes, like birettas, were essentially liturgical and domestic garments; not social ones.

It was a black, straight-cut, narrow-skirted cassock without monsignorial magenta piping or cincture, which he wore an inch or so above the ankle, after the style of the Fathers at the London (Brompton) Oratory.

In any case, he believed that once one accepted membership of a self-governing institution like a London club, then by definition one also accepted that institution's codes and usages – even when, as in this instance, they were unwritten. As he once pointed out to a friend at the Travellers', who was intent upon an act of single-handed mutiny, individual club members are not at liberty to follow only those rules which are personally congenial to them. 'What you can do, however, and I urge you to do so, is to try to reverse this woeful decision[m] at the next House Committee Meeting.'

Alfred's outward tolerance of norms and notions which potentially conflicted with his own convictions and sensibilities went far wider and deeper than any conforming instinct. His toleration was

[l] The Rev. Dr John Ludlow Lopes (1880–1960); Chaplain to undergraduates at Cambridge (1922–28), to whom Alfred had been devoted since his own charmed undergraduate years at Trinity. Under Lopes he had been President of the Fisher Society.

[m] It had been decided, I seem to recall, to introduce paper towels into the club's cloakrooms. The mutiny would have involved the use of a portable shredding machine. At the next House Committee, after much canvassing, the 'woeful' decision was indeed reversed. Needless to say, some years later the Anti-Paperists lost their battle.

rooted in the knowledge that human society is a divided house. He quietly insisted, however, that such divisions were not of themselves necessarily synonymous with acrimony. It was fallen man, at once arrogant and pusillanimous, who made them so. At our last meeting he rehearsed this thesis:

> Human folly and villainy are boundless because they are intrinsic to our condition. But no one race or cultural tradition and still less one social class or government can be accused, even Stalin's, as being *more* inherently evil, or for that matter better than another. As always, my dear Peter, good and evil, and everything which flows from these two impulses, can only be appraised in the context of individual choice.

Theology apart, this conviction was the fruit of Alfred's own human experience. Both as a man and as a priest he had dallied and laboured in a thousand gardens.

King George V is described as having 'spanned the centuries'.[2] Alfred spanned society; not admittedly the whole social arc, yet sizeable segments of it. This had happened in the first place because of his own many-faceted family and social background. Later, as a priest with a wide cure of souls, it became more or less inevitable. He first spent thirty-three years as Catholic chaplain at Cambridge, and then thirty-two in London continuing the same work which his retirement from Fisher House in 1965 had only very temporarily interrupted. In all, a pastoral cure which lasted sixty-five years.

That Alfred was able to slip from one social group or situation to another without ever appearing insincere or superficial was the result of an innate talent to empathise. He also made people laugh and, indeed, love each other. Moreover, because they instantly became the cynosure of his attention, he made people feel important too.

In such situations, while his mind delved and his voice evoked and wove patterns of the past before one, his heart was living for the moment – that moment – in which he made you his co-protagonist, his fellow conspirator. But at the same time you knew, or at any rate

you felt, that his soul was already walking in eternity. And this
sensation also contributed to the success of his personal relationships, for it created in his interlocutors a feeling of security as well as
the hope that one day they too might attain a similar condition of
spiritual serenity and worldly detachment.

Loyal to his mother's routine,[n] which he had followed since the
placid, halcyon years at Mark Hall, Alfred used to say his Rosary
most evenings, between seven and eight. Whenever appropriate,[o]
his guests at dinner would be invited to join him. Essentially of
course a devotional exercise, these occasions – and they were also
precisely that: *occasions* – epitomised this evocative nexus of past,
present and future time, which was not merely the hallmark but the
very cornerstone of Alfred's communion with others.

Whether before the altar in his pocket-sized chapel at the Travellers', or by the library fire at Rose Hill, or on an early evening
train to Cambridge, saying the Rosary with Alfred was a social and
pastoral experience as well as a spiritual exercise.

Paradoxical though it may sound, it can be argued that Alfred's
social success and 'mobility' was also a measure of his detachment.
He participated, enthusiastically or dutifully, in half a dozen or
more distinct, if frequently overlapping, ambiences, but he never
wholly belonged to any one of them. Neither kinsman nor close
friend, Englishman or Spaniard, scholar or beagler, aesthete or
clubman could claim Alfred as entirely theirs. As he once pointed
out, 'I am sociable not gregarious', meaning 'gregarious' literally –
one of a flock, a crowd. Under God, he was his own man. He was
also a priest with a covenanted obligation – 'ut nullis perturbation-
ibus impediti, liberam servitutem tuis semper exhibeamus officiis'.
But if in the last analysis he was the most independent and private
of men, he was seldom self-preoccupied or indifferent. Even at his
most aloof, Alfred's charm never abandoned him for long. And his

[n] Maria Victorina would gather her sons and daughters about her chair, and in
rapid Spanish fashion they rattled through their beads. Alfred recalled: 'I was
always trying to slow us down.' English liturgical propriety attempting to curb
Spanish spontaneity.
[o] Alfred was, as he averred, 'socially ecumenical': not all his guests were Catholics.

curiosity was on occasions as feline as his affections were deeply felt and enduring.

Our own friendship, which had begun with such an eruption of mutual trust and spontaneous affection, soon steadied. Apart from any other consideration, there was a book to be written. It would become 'my' book, yet without Alfred's contribution the enterprise could easily founder. Clear heads constituted a *sine qua non*, while warm hearts gave us the emotional zest. So, with the book's gestation providing, as it were, the splints for the strengthening bones of friendship, our task went ahead with purpose and an ever more pronounced complicity.

Nevertheless, Alfred was not easy to get to know. He was suave and friendly and familiar, but seldom intimate. He would tell endless stories about himself – funny stories usually, and as often as not shrewdly commented upon, but I had to glean for myself the self-knowledge these anecdotes revealed. Even at his most genial and apparently confidential, Alfred was also elusive. No doubt this was a question of character. But his reluctance, or indeed his inability, to talk about his own feelings and emotions *directly* was a matter of generation too. Upper-class Edwardian reticence was no mere pose: it had been a behavioural ground-rule. 'One' just didn't. And while, to some extent, Alfred shied against this (though very quietly of course), he complied as well.

Fortunately, none of this seemed to matter very much. With the result that our growing intimacy was almost never noticeably impeded. However, the difference of generation and social class existed, and the outcome was as probably inevitable as I found it also 'all very right and proper' (a favourite Alfredian phrase). I became his pupil.

While our subsequent conversation-supervisions were possibly for Alfred 'ordinary admin' – he had already spent a working lifetime doing very much the same manner of thing – for me they were a delicious novelty. Because Alfred did not simply evoke and describe the past, as for example my grandmother had done (adding another, and magical, dimension to an already charmed childhood), he explained its workings and justified the religious and socio-political tenets upon which earlier orderings of society had been based. In a phrase, Alfred provided intellectual cogency. He made the past speak intelligibly, so that my own long and dearly held *opinions* were at last given an ideological framework.

At the same time we laughed and joked a great deal, though never, I think, for the sake of the thing. Alfred possessed a fine turn of whimsy, but he eschewed frivolity. Rather, we laughed at some story or remembered episode which illustrated or followed on from what we had been saying. And this shared sense and style of humour enforced and confirmed our mutual convictions. We were thoroughly at ease in each other's company.

I was, however, always conscious that there were intrinsic limits to our friendship. It could probably not have been otherwise. The most significant was the result of Alfred's being a priest and, especially, a priest who had been trained and ordained in an age of church history when detachment from the laity was still regarded as a sacerdotal virtue.

Although Alfred's warmth and ebullience, coupled with his talent for making friends, tended to disguise the fact, he did in the last analysis subscribe to the Pre-Conciliar ordering of relationships between a priest and his flock. This was never more apparent than when attending one of Alfred's Masses, however intimate the physical surroundings. In the Travellers' his chapel measured perhaps no more than ten feet by eight. During those fleeting seconds in the Tridentine Rite when the celebrant turns from the altar to face his congregation, hardly a flicker of recognition would escape from Alfred's faraway gaze. Just minutes earlier we would have been chuckling over some gentle absurdity.

But once vested, Alfred the friend and counsellor seemed to dissolve behind the veils of ecclesiastical propriety. Suddenly remote and austere – shoulders flexed in a visible effort to correct their tendency to stoop, the eyes hooded and shadowy, long hands like blotched marble replicas of themselves – Alfred would celebrate the Sacred Mysteries with all the inscrutable fervour of a counter-Reformation prince-bishop. Initially this transformation unnerved me; presumptuously, I also felt somehow rejected. However, I eventually realised that it was not principally respect for traditional liturgical decorum which determined this transformation, but rather his own need to disconnect himself from his immediate surroundings, lest his earthly affections for those for whom he was saying Mass might deflect his and indeed our own attention from the workings of divine love, at a moment when one is potentially most exposed to its saving grace.

'I only hope, however,' Alfred replied to me when I once voiced these misgivings after serving his Mass at which I had been his only congregation, 'that my behaviour at the altar doesn't appear ostentatious or, Heaven forbid, "put on".' As at the time I assured him, perhaps somewhat backhandedly, that once one understood the reasons behind his behaviour, then it couldn't possibly be misconstrued, it seems only right that Alfred should be given the last word: 'No one can receive the sublime and awful grace of the priesthood without fear and trembling. Some things lose their awe with familiarity; not so the priesthood.'

'Now I want a full report about it all, and whatever else you say, don't leave out how you felt about the thing.' As a friend, Alfred's interest in me and my doings was spontaneous and wholehearted.

At the same time, he exerted immense emotional restraint. There were times when I could practically hear the questions he left unasked. But circumspection had by then become a way of life, no longer merely a rule of gentlemanly behaviour. Nevertheless, whenever I confided in Alfred or sought his advice, he would suddenly unwind. And if as a man he was easily embarrassed, especially where sexual matters were concerned (as inevitably they often were), as a priest he was utterly undeterred. Indeed he positively flouted that circumspection of expression which otherwise characterised his dealings with others. And this became even more marked when I asked Alfred whether he would instruct me. 'Of course I shall. You can't imagine how long and how hard I've prayed for this. We've been friends, more than friends; but now … the sky's the limit.'

'Truth alone is worthy of our entire devotion.' This lapidary axiom of Fr Vincent McNabb's, O.P., was not only a sentiment which found its echo at the very core of Alfred's humanity, it transposed into words the cornerstone upon which his entire priestly ministry was based.

In many ways Alfred was at his absolute best during those hour-or-so sessions when he was preparing me to be received. He was as charming and as courteous as ever; but now the priest emerged fully from the man, revealing the tempered steel of an intellect freed from the social constraints which giving or receiving hospitality imply. While he displayed his usual patience and empathy, there was little else left of the urbane prelate who smiled and demurred over the claret and candlelight. Never a moment of self-deprecation – for indeed his 'self' was barely a part of these proceedings – as he explicated not only the Church of Rome's fundamental dogmas, but also digressed, less austerely perhaps but no less succinctly, upon the secular accretions of pious belief and devotional custom. 'For you see, Peter, as dogma encapsulates revealed Truth, so pious beliefs flow from, and bear witness to, that same Truth. Take for instance holy water stoops. When I was a child, the good Jesuit fathers who came to Mark Hall from Farm Street would remind us that Holy Mother Church had decreed that good Catholics were to dip their first two fingers into the stoop and make the sign of the cross as soon as they *entered* a church. It was, however, the older members of my family who made sure that we performed this same act of devotion upon *leaving* our chapel. A perfect example of the osmosis between the official and the unofficial; between a rule of devotional homage and decorum laid down by ecclesiastical authority, and a consequential act of piety invented by the laity.'

If Alfred's style and manner of expounding the Catholic Faith veered towards the idiosyncratic, the substance of his course of instructions was unerringly and implacably orthodox. 'Once you accept the incarnation as the cardinal and over-arching Christian mystery, then, by God's grace, you're home and dry. Believe that, and, again by God's grace, everything else Holy Church sees fit to teach will follow on automatically, and will not only make sense to your reason, but also your heart and soul will *know* that Christian Truth embodies the essence of all sense.'

Alfred's approach was straightforwardly didactic. Assuming, and in my case perfectly correctly, that anyone who asked for instruction wanted precisely that and not, for example, an exchange of theological opinions, Alfred never asked me for mine. Rather; 'If you're not clear on any particular point, tell me and I'll try to explain it another way.'

This was in relief-making contrast to an earlier experience when I had sought instruction. Then, the priest had kept asking me why I wanted to become a Catholic, with the result that there were moments when I almost felt that I was instructing him. This continued for several increasingly fraught weeks, until the day I answered, or rather 'asked' back: 'Father, shouldn't it be *you* telling *me* why I must ... join your Church?'

With Alfred holding and dealing the doctrinal cards, neither I nor any other instructee risked such a sense of frustration or disappointment. Alfred also made it clear that one was at total liberty to interrupt his course of instructions, or to withdraw from them altogether, at any moment whatsoever. Moreover, there would be no discussion or, still less, personal offence or hard feelings on Alfred's part. 'I am a humble, I hope, instrument in the hands of Almighty God; not some haughty viceroy from the Heavenly Kingdom.'

We would meet in his bedroom at the Travellers', usually between teatime and dinner. The routine was reassuringly unvaried during those spring and summer late afternoons (from May to October 1977), with the blinds drawn down and the room cocooned from the world in a golden glow. The mingled aromas of furniture polish, dust and Pear's soap[p] permeated the warm, dry air. Alfred would sit in a high-backed leather armchair with his sister Carmen's old back-board resting on its arms. A foot or so away, I perched less comfortably but as contented as a sandboy on a rickety bedroom chair with a Viennese straw seat. Alfred's legs would be stretched out in front of him, ankles crossed. When he wasn't reading aloud from one of the books extracted from the little pile

---

[p] 'David [Watkin] says my room smells of pepper. He's probably right. What do you think?' Alfred once asked me rather absently while he pared and buffed his nails before going out to celebrate Mass at Farm Street.

on the carpet, his eyes would usually be closed, while he held his
spectacles flat between those long fingers.

With the surrounding silence providing a soft backdrop to his
low, rapid speech (Alfred murmured, never mumbled), he talked
with apparent effortlessness from start to finish, and certainly with
no interruption on my part. But although I was entranced, I was
able to register the points Alfred was making. Such was the spell he
wove: one was both lulled and yet alert.

Despite the agreeable surroundings and what many would consider a highly rarefied social context, Alfred's narrative skills caused
the tumultuous realities of the first century AD to break through to
the exclusion of all else. For although he read out passages from
such authors as R. H. Benson, Belloc and Chesterton, as well as
Douglas Woodruff and even Housman and Eric Gill, to illustrate
the Church's social doctrine, along with lyrical extracts from
Bishop Challoner's *The Garden of the Soul* (1740) on questions of
devotion, when he was recounting events from the life of Christ he
spoke with all the immediacy and barely suppressed emotion of an
eyewitness. In those moments it was as if the long centuries of an
all-powerful Church were as yet to come. Instead he transported
one, body and soul, to the very foot of the Cross, evoking first the
tormented deliberations of Pilate and the anguished flight of St
Peter, the tears of Our Lady, and finally to the blood and dust of the
Crucifixion itself. He spoke with the sincerity of the suffering
believer.

But as soon as we had finished the voice from the Judean desert
vanished as if borne away by the same wind-devils it had previously
challenged. 'Peter, if you'd go down to the Smoking Room and
order us two glasses of sherry, I'll join you directly.'

Coupled with Alfred's ultimate reserve and, I believe, to a certain
extent underpinning it, was his sharp but invariably amused understanding of English social nuance, and of the snobberies of class
and cadre in particular. His immediate family was not landowning
gentry (Mark Hall itself was rented). Their prosperity was based on
(the wine) trade. It was the magnitude of their fortune, coupled
with their gentlemanly tastes and pursuits which had assured their

acceptance into the society of rural Essex. Alfred's father was a member of the Carlton Club, not of White's or Boodle's. The family was devoutly and stoutly Roman Catholic, but there were no recusant forebears. No Elizabethan or Georgian Gilbey lay at rest in a family chapel. Of all this Alfred was as aware in the early 1920s, when it mattered far more, as he was seventy years later. Awareness did not, however, lead to any discernible resentment. Besides, his aesthetic sensibilities set him apart from a broad swathe of the English upper class with whom he might be expected to be socially at home, not to mention the overwhelming majority of later twentieth century churchmen, Romans and Anglicans alike, 'who', Alfred once commented, 'commission their unappealing "church and parish complexes" and are well pleased. So they can't possibly be aware of the damage they are doing. Or can they? One hopes not.'

In response to the charge of proselytism, Alfred told one journalist: 'Conversion? No, I've never done that. I receive. I instruct.'[3] He could have added 'I never instigate.' On the same theme he suggested to another interviewer: 'Call me when you're ready; human nature works best that way.'[4] This policy of studied *laisser aller* not only informed Alfred's priestly approach to would-be converts, it also conditioned his more purely social dealings. Take, for instance, heraldry – something that had enthralled him since childhood. With me he never broached the subject. I did once or twice ask him some specific question, which he answered with alacrity and precision. We had other and mutual fields of interest, and those we explored endlessly. I am sure, however, that had I asked for a full-blown course of Heraldic Instruction, then he would have obliged – and with even greater alacrity. Alfred never imposed himself, unless as a priest he was under obligation to do so. Instead – welcoming as well as merely recognising the rich conversational potential of the variegated milieux in which he moved – he preferred to steer the conversation towards subjects which the assembled company would be likely to find spontaneously congenial.

What commanded Alfred's intellectual attention and emotional interest was that kind of free-ranging intercourse between individuals, where anecdote mingled with comment and flights of fantasy merged with opinion and personal recollection. It was to this he was alluding when he stood up in the Hall at Trinity College, Cambridge, at the conclusion of a dinner to celebrate the fortieth anniversary of his ordination and recounted[5] to those present that:

> This seems a singularly inappropriate occasion to make the claim, but I am really a very private person; so what I should have liked would not have been one dinner of 170 persons, but 170 successive dinners at which I could have dined *à deux* with each of you in turn. Then indeed we might have 'tired the sun with talking'.[6]

The following week we were drinking tea at the Over-Seas League in St James's Place, and reading aloud the reports of the Trinity dinner in the Catholic papers. Christopher Howse's piece in *The Universe* had particularly captured Alfred's attention. 'Oh my goodness, did I really say that? – "One hundred and seventy successive dinners ..." What a horribly greedy old man "Father Mac Murphy" and his dear, good parishioners must be saying of me. I am of course. Extremely greedy – and indolent too. Christopher[q] is naughty though, even if, God bless the boy, his intentions are always of the best. Not much I can do about it now, I suppose. Except say my prayers.'

That between 'Father Mac Murphy' and Alfred there was a social, cultural and presumably generational abyss really goes without saying. But there would have been no fundamental religious differences. Their pastoral approach and the style and manner of their liturgical presentation no doubt varied considerably, but they were both priests in the same Church: the faith they preached and in whose name they prayed embraced them with an identical promise. Two souls; one God. In the same way, the majority of Father Mac Murphy's parishioners will have moved in circles vastly removed from the majority of Alfred's friends and flock. However,

---

[q] Not Howse, but the Hon. Christopher Monckton, at that time editor of *The Universe*, and a son of one of Alfred's oldest friends Major-General Viscount Monckton of Brenchley, co-founder of the Strafford Club in 1939 with Alfred, the Duke of Rutland, the historian Brian Wormald of Peterhouse and others.

both groups – millions in the former, several hundreds in the latter – share a common loyalty. The ethos of their devotions may differ, though not the content.

The twentieth century's egalitarian and collectivist tendencies have upset the previous formal hierarchies, and removed most of those privileges once sanctioned exclusively by birth or rank, but human societies everywhere remain pyramidal. And England's large Catholic minority has proved no exception. So ultimately the distinctions, both real and imaginary, between the worlds represented on the one hand by the average parish and on the other by a university or a private chapel (and precious few of the latter remain) are, religiously speaking, as unimportant as they are, statistically, inevitable. A myriad separate voices and different accents singing in a thousand choirs which invoke, however, a single Mystery.

What does matter though, and which here concerns us intimately, is how these distinctions were often wheeled out and used against Alfred's priestly ministry. For there existed a body of opinion amongst some of those who wrote about Alfred during the concluding decade and a half of his life, which argued that he cared only and prayed only for those of high birth and ample private means.

Anyone who knew Alfred even only moderately well would be likely to query such an accusation. For those who knew him better – and so very few of his true intimates were either seriously rich or, in the traditional usage of the term, 'well born' – the charge is an insult.

Considered generously, this is an erroneous reading based on flawed logic, and is as fatuous as proposing that Anglican archdeacons love buildings and not people because their jobs centre upon the upkeep of Church property. To suggest that Alfred was a snobbish prelate who carried out his priestly duties so assiduously *only because* his flock were members of a 'privileged élite' is to misunderstand Alfred himself and to misconstrue his life's work.

When in 1932 he was appointed Roman Catholic Chaplain at Cambridge, he found there a ready-made society in whose creation he had played no part, nor ever was to. He was moreover under sacerdotal obligation to provide this undergraduate flock, whoever they were, wherever they 'came from', and whatever they were like personally, with as complete a cure as 'circumstances permit'. And this he did, for a hundred terms, to the limits of his talents and personal fortune. Happily, both were considerable. So that when he left Fisher House, if there were members of his former flock who rallied enthusiastically to the new incumbent, others sought Alfred out in London and urged him to continue there the cure of their souls. At the age of sixty-five he took up their challenge. He could so easily have slipped into sequestered retirement as his friend and sometime Oxford counterpart, Mgr Ronald Knox, had done some twenty years earlier.

'I could no more have translated the Bible than you, my dear Tertius,[r] are going to persuade me to drink a single drop more of this excellent champagne. They say Ronnie's Latin was better than Horace's. Whereas I have no scholarship whatsoever. I'm a bog-priest by comparison.'

None the less, it is a charming though somewhat disconcerting thought that Alfred might have spent the last thirty-three years of his life (always assuming he survived the rigours and the relative isolation) as resident chaplain at a boys' preparatory school in deepest Suffolk.

Commander Peregrine Hubbard, the headmaster of Moreton Hall near Bury, and his wife Lady Miriam, extended their well-meant invitation during the winter of 1966. 'I think I realised right from the start', Lady Miriam recalled for me, 'that our offer was not on.'

> Of course Alfred was charm itself; he even stayed to boys' tea. You see, we both admire him so very much, and at the time felt jolly sorry about how shabbily he'd been treated. Alfred told us about the whole business, and said that the Cardinal had been most courteous and correct. I daresay he was. But then Alfred never does blame other people.
>
> He conquered me, you know, when I was a teenager. He used to stay with us in the north, on his way between

[r] Tertius Metcalfe (1931–96). We were his guests at Henley that year.

Stonyhurst and Ampleforth. His beautiful table manners put
my own to shame. He could break a piece of toast into perfect
halves without letting drop a single crumb. But what I most
loved was watching him peel an apple. He produced from
some invisible pocket a little silver folding fruit-knife, like a
well-bred conjurer.

I told her that Alfred was still an impeccable peeler of apples.

So Alfred did not rusticate in Suffolk; he stayed in London, to
welcome back his flock. As the years passed, and many of the traditional practices of parish Catholicism passed with them, so his flock
multiplied, as increasing numbers of the disenchanted and disori-
entated gravitated into Alfred's new pastoral orbit. Had Alfred not
been available to receive them, it is more than likely that many
would have been lost to the Church. If there were those amongst
them who were attracted as much by the man as by the religion he
represented – by his panache and *politesse*, by his social aplomb
and his serene yet implacable orthodoxy – Alfred himself was
essentially indifferent about the reasons for his popularity. He
never courted it, but neither did he take it for granted – 'I am an
instrument in the hands of Almighty God, that's all.' Or, as Eamon
Duffy puts it: 'Alfred Gilbey was a man of disarming simplicity, in
whom social decorum blended indistinguishably into the life of
grace.'[7] As it was, he simply made himself as available as he could.
There were minds to be guided and souls to be nurtured.

Alfred's visits to the sick and dying were more frequent than
many realised. An urgent request would be relayed to him, and he
would respond as urgently, slipping hurriedly out of the Travellers'
at all hours of the day and night. Such calls on his time and wan-
ing physical reserves obviously tired him. Simultaneously they
refreshed his spirit and sharpened his priestly resolve.

That there was a social as well as a spiritual dimension to
Alfred's cure of souls was an added bonus for all concerned. With a
handful of his flock he had always shared a social background. But
it was with many that he shared similar tastes and interests. As a
result, friendships were struck and cherished.

Alfred often entertained his friends; less frequently did *they* manage to return his largesse. This was for no lack of trying on their part. When it was practically always Alfred who got up from the table and extracted the company-sized Barclays cheque book from his coat-tails as he strolled in the direction of the cashier, his excuses were two. He was richer than most of us, which was doubtless true enough – 'I'd rather that my friends ate my money than the State confiscate it when I'm dead.' Second, that in his opinion he was a better host than guest – 'I usually end up misbehaving myself.' This was of course a delicious fib. He was as gracious a guest as he was a punctilious and generous host.

The entertaining helped to make Alfred's work and his life in general more agreeable. It was not, though, the fuel which powered the mill. For the mill ran on religion – on Trent wine and numinous discs of imprinted rice bread, not on claret or roast woodcock. So to insist otherwise – whether wilfully or ingenuously – is to confuse personal taste and preferences with professional and priestly obligations; and ultimately, to ignore the distinction between liking and loving. Alfred, the upper class Englishman who admired beauty and respected excellence, most certainly enjoyed the company of intelligent, personable and well-mannered men who shared his own political, social and aesthetic outlook. But as a priest, he took no notice whatsoever of social status, except to point out that high birth and worldly possessions conferred neither spiritual privileges nor a better bargaining position for heavenly rewards. He would sometimes quote Ronald Knox on the subject:

> I am not going to decide whether the average Catholic Mexican is what you [Sir Arnold Lunn] call 'a better man' than the average Protestant Englishman. I do not know – I know which I would rather go for a walking tour with, but that is not the same thing. I prefer Englishmen … but that is not going to do them much good, poor dears, at the Day of Judgement.[8]

Similarly, Alfred would point out that the rooms he had furnished or embellished at Fisher House, or later at the Travellers' and at Rose Hill, were no better *morally* than Father Mac Murphy's priest house and parish hall. He just happened to find the former more to his personal liking – 'altogether a different matter'.

If then Alfred brought to his priestcraft, and to the environs where he practised it, the ethos and material effects of a rich and conservative-minded gentleman-aesthete, how much had Catholicism, in its turn, contributed to the person he was to become? 'In a superficial sense', Alfred confided to me one frosty January lunchtime, 'absolutely nothing. Otherwise everything – the whole works. Until I went to the Beda and gave away all my pretty clothes, I was indistinguishable. Only my family and a few intimates knew, or guessed, exactly how greatly Holy Mother Church conditioned all my thoughts, and determined the way I behaved. I am law-abiding by nature. But the awareness of mortal sin was a far more effective deterrent.' He told one interviewer that even as a boy he realised that the England which he knew and loved and the Catholic Church were two aspects of the same civilisation, and that he wanted to increase the communication between the one and the other. Or, as he told me that frosty lunchtime, 'to Catholicise and to Englishise at the same time – I was a very presumptuous boy indeed.'

Clothes for Alfred were also a source of intimate amusement and private association. Once, going down the drive at Rose Hill, it was pointed out to him that his silk handkerchief was poking out of his tailcoat pocket, and the concerned friend spontaneously sought to push it back inside. 'Oh, no, no. Thank you so much. It's perfectly all right where it is.' We paused, but when no further word of explanation was forthcoming, the conversation continued as the four of us walked on. What image, what scene or archetype was in Alfred's mind? Whatever it was, it was evidently both very real and very dear to him. Otherwise he would never have been so brusque or enigmatic.

Alfred on Henley Saturday, amused and radiant, in a speckled boater tilted with Beerbohmesque élan; Alfred arriving for the Opening of Parliament in top hat and silk-faced frock-coat; Alfred out beagling, standing on the edge of a fenceless East Anglian field, with the low winter sun painting the stubble a still deeper shade of crimson than the lining of his black hacking jacket; or again, Alfred flitting down a hushed midnight corridor in a white lawn nightshirt; Alfred resplendent in *cappa magna* or brocaded cope, aquiline and Hispanic, a Cardinal Pirelli figure, processing towards the high altar at the Oratory, with his upper lip drawn down at the corners and his biretta worn low on his forehead. A hundred and other such vignettes come to mind. But none seems to me more evocative of Alfred's idiosyncratic elegance and sartorial sense of humour than the scene which presented itself one hot August afternoon in the library at Rose Hill. Alfred was dozing over his breviary, with his father's old spectacles on the very tip of his nose. He had discarded his cassock immediately after lunch, and was now sitting in a collarless shirt of black and cream striped silk, black breeches with Pitt Club silver knee-buttons, black lisle stockings and buckled shoes. Had Gainsborough or Reynolds ridden over to paint the picture, they would have found nothing missing except an ecclesiastical wig; a beautifully powdered wig it would have been, arranged on its cedarwood stand, within convenient reaching-distance of the old prelate's chair. But on this quintessential occasion, the man himself emerged as always from the folds, flaps and buckles of the clothes he wore: detached yet engaged, absorbed but aware.

Alfred was elegant and impeccable; his hosiers, tailors and cutters were master craftsmen. But while these accidentals gave Alfred considerable personal pleasure and satisfaction, he was alive to the fact that there was more at stake than socio-aesthetics. For he knew that the image he projected could inspire and cajole, especially those of his flock who fretted and complained about 'the way the Church is going today'. 'If my starched cuffs and all this' – his narrow-sleeved arm and glance briefly embraced the Coffee Room at the Travellers', where twenty or thirty dark-suited diners sat at tables where the mahogany shone and the silver winked in the candlelight – 'if this will help me, with God's grace, to bring one single soul to the sacraments, then Alfred Gilbey will not have worked entirely in vain.' Shades of Pope Pius XI – abroad in Pall Mall.

It was almost as a shade that I last saw Alfred Gilbey, as his retreating figure walked, somewhat haltingly and heavily stooped, in and out of the orange glare of the street lamps as he made his slow progress to the Travellers'. A world away, it seemed, from that riveting, relaxed trio on King's Parade, Cambridge. We had been dining *à deux* at the Oxford and Cambridge on a September night six months before he died, and nearly twenty-two years after our first meal there. I stood on the steps of the club and watched him go. Not because I was stricken by any premonition as such, for Alfred had talked non-stop all evening, had eaten heartily and more than enjoyed the claret and port we had drunk. Rather because, in the 'logic' of the thing, this could so easily have been our last meeting. And indeed so it was.

SOURCE NOTES

1 A. N. Wilson, 'Divine Right' in *Harpers & Queen*, April 1984.

2 Kenneth Rose, *King George V*, Weidenfeld & Nicolson, 1983, p. xiii.

3 To John Mortimer, who described himself in the same piece as a 'devout' atheist, writing for *The Spectator*, 6 July 1991.

4 To Glenys Roberts, publisher of *The Commonplace Book of Monsignor A.N. Gilbey*, Libri Mundi, 1993; in 'Keeping Faith', *Sunday Telegraph*, 30 June 1993.

5 For the complete text of this scintillating speech, see *The Fisher House Newsletter*, 1979.

6 'how often you and I / Had tired the sun with talking and sent him down the sky.' William Johnson Cory (1823–92), 'Heraclitus'.

7 Eamon Duffy, Reader in Church History at the University of Cambridge, in 'Eyewitness', *The Tablet*, 11–18 April 1998.

8 Ronald Knox and Arnold Lunn, *Difficulties*, 1932, p. 229, quoted in Evelyn Waugh, *Ronald Knox*, 1959.

Charles Hargrove

ALFRED NEWMAN GILBEY: A TRIBUTE

I met Alfred Gilbey shortly after I went up to Cambridge, at the beginning of the Lent Term 1941. My father had obtained an introduction for me through David Mathew, then auxiliary bishop of Westminster, and had also written to inform Alfred of my coming up. He received in return one of the very few letters I have ever seen in Alfred's neat copperplate hand, suggesting I call at Fisher House as soon as I took up residence at Peterhouse. This I did. I can remember nothing about that historic first meeting, save that it was marked by the utmost cordiality. It was the beginning of a firm friendship of more than fifty years, until his death in March 1998.

My contacts with him after I went down were necessarily intermittent, particularly during my six and a half years' posting as correspondent of *The Times* in Japan, and an equally long spell in Germany after that. But we always kept in touch, rarely by correspondence but through my occasional visits to Cambridge and after 1965 to London, when he always received me with the warmest and most decorous hospitality. I recall on one occasion at least, before he had had to give up the Chaplaincy after thirty-three years, being extended the honours of the 'bishop's room', the best bedroom of Fisher House, with its rich damask furnishings; and enjoying the ministrations of Glockner, the butler and handyman, and the fare prepared by Mrs Glockner, his French wife from Béziers, who took to me all the more because of my French mother. In fact, we used to converse in the language not of Racine or Chateaubriand, but rather of Marcel Pagnol, the immortal creator of *Marius*.

The couple were utterly devoted to Alfred Gilbey. Glockner

himself was a rather colourless and conventional Scotsman, a perfect 'gentleman's gentleman', of no particular views that I could ever ascertain. But Mrs Glockner was an enthusiastic supporter of the Communist cause in Britain, a sort of kindlier Madame Defarge, whom it was hard to imagine knitting at the foot of the guillotine and counting the heads as they fell in the basket. I remember Alfred telling me she had once reassured him that when the '*grand soir*', the Revolution, broke out – which could only be a matter of time – he would be spared the wrath of the victorious proletariat; for what reasons was not clear, beyond the fact that even ardent Communists had human weaknesses. When, in due course, Glockner died and Mrs Glockner, who had soldiered on for a while after he was gone, fell prey to a number of ills, Alfred had her installed in a home where she was miserable, and always complained of her fate. But he would dutifully visit her once a week and reminisce with her about happier times, however boring the old woman's conversation must undoubtedly have been. It sheds a touching light on a trait of his character which many of those of his circle were not privileged to see – his kindness and loyalty to those who had been in his service and loyal to him.

I became part of his 'flock', as he liked to call it, and Fisher House was open to me, as to all others who belonged to it, at almost all hours for spiritual guidance, confession or the more worldly pleasures of conversation and discussion in the handsome long room on the first floor, and in the dining room where the portraits revealed his Jacobite convictions. There was no telephone in sight: that was concealed in a cupboard under some bookshelves, next to his armchair on one side of the fireplace. If it rang, the cupboard would be opened and a weirdly anachronistic instrument on a tall stand arm and with a separate earphone would be revealed. When its intrusion was not welcomed, it would simply go unanswered.

His religion was not austere or melancholy, but completely serene. Behind the elegant façade, the social banter and the touch of eccentricity, there was a genuine modesty, more than a measure of holiness and a real austerity. When he had become Protonotary

Apostolic, he wore his purple so discreetly that it was almost invisible to the casual eye. But he was very proud of his scarlet socks, which, he told me, came from a famous supplier to the Roman Curia. On one occasion he asked me up to his bedroom as he was preparing to go out to dinner. I was surprised to discover a monastic cell, with whitewashed walls, sparsely furnished, with a chest of drawers, a wardrobe, a couple of chairs and an iron bedstead with a horsehair mattress. The only worldly touch was a pair of riding boots in a corner – evidence of his lifelong enthusiasm for hunting. Here it was that one had the revelation, beyond the sophisticated priest and prelate, an other-worldly Alfred Gilbey, a genuine man of God.

I was privileged on many occasions to serve his Mass at Fisher House. Each time it was a moving experience. He pronounced the words of the liturgy with immense feeling and conviction. I recall vividly his manner of saying the Lord's Prayer. He spoke to God in almost conversational tone, and his pronunciation of Latin was distinctly Continental. One felt that every one of his Masses was for him a privileged occasion to meet a loving Lord and Master who was also an old friend.

It was inevitable that – as with all men of strong personality and character at odds with their times – he was the subject of controversy. His views were often misunderstood and misrepresented, especially in the context of 'political correctness'. He was criticised for his rejection of the notion of equality of the sexes and his steadfast opposition to the admission of women to the Chaplaincy. His grounds for so doing were simple: they had their own chaplain to minister to their individual needs. He was emphatically no misogynist: in his view women were not the equals of, but different from men. My French wife always found great pleasure and intellectual stimulation in his company, and their conversation sometimes lapsed into French, of which he had an impressive command. The issue cast a cloud over his last years at Cambridge. When the Catholic hierarchy overruled him and reluctantly asked him to leave – a year before the term he had set himself – he obeyed with sadness and dignity. It turned out to be the starting point of an equally rich and rewarding and enduring apostolate in London, from his abode at the Travellers' Club.

Alfred Gilbey's substantial private means enabled him to keep open house for his friends and the friends of his friends, or even complete strangers who had an introduction to him; and to entertain them in style. He did so after Mass on Sundays, when his sherry flowed liberally, or at Trinity, his old college, where he was always much in demand; or at the Bath Hotel, an old coaching inn, now vanished, close to the Chaplaincy. In an article which appeared in *The Times* after his death, which gave a wholly misleading and distinctly critical impression of his personality and his ministry, it was alleged that Fisher House was some kind of stronghold of recusancy and of Jacobite nostalgia frequented by the scions of the 'Old Catholick' families, and more than a sprinkling of the aristocratic establishment.

I can only speak for myself. I was not an 'Old Catholick', having been brought up in Paris in a solidly middle-class context. My family background was liberal, not Jacobite or even High Tory, and my father was an agnostic, though thanks to my French mother I had been brought up a Catholic. My outlook was perforce cosmopolitan, like Alfred Gilbey's, despite his very English opinions and tastes. But from the outset I felt at ease and at home. And I was no exception. His door was open to all – 'Catholicks', more contemporary-style 'Romans', Protestants, agnostics, and even unbelievers, drawn from the upper, middle and lower classes, who all received the same welcome and were equally attracted by the warm and civilised atmosphere. His convictions, his views about life and society, his conception of higher education and its role of turning out Christian gentlemen, whatever their social backgrounds, his hostility to all forms of egalitarianism and 'liberal humanism' – these were all stoutly held but always charitably expressed. This was not always the case with those who claimed to be his admirers and disciples. And he was tolerant of honest dissent. In matters of religion he was an uncompromising traditionalist, faithful to the last of the Mass of St Pius V, which he had a special faculty from the Archbishop of Westminster to celebrate daily. But always he remained obedient to papal authority and was never remotely tempted to support the Lefèbvrist schism, though sympathetic to many of its strictures of post-Vatican II excesses and aberrations.

His dress, his tastes, his views on men and manners were also traditional and reflected his preference for the ways of a more gracious age and more stable society. But he did not wallow in nostalgia. His approach to literature was eclectic, with a special fondness for Trollope and Mrs Humphry Ward. Unlike many Catholic clergy, he understood and appreciated the unique contribution of Anglicanism to English culture over the past four centuries, whether in thought, art, music or the vernacular ritual. He often encouraged me to go to King's Chapel for what he called 'the concert', on the grounds that it was a uniquely uplifting experience.

He liked pomp and circumstance, on the grounds that nothing was too splendid for God. But he disliked pomposity and self-importance. His criticism of others, when called for, was always measured and charitable. I never saw him speak in anger. Above all, he brought to his life, as both a man and a priest, a genuine *joie de vivre*. And there was nothing he liked better than a dinner with friends, with good food, good wine, and good talk. I remember his delightful sense of humour and his fondness for anecdotes, whether his own or those of others, which he would punctuate with a high-pitched laugh.

Jocelyn Hillgarth

I first met Alfred Gilbey in 1949 when I was in my second year at Cambridge, reading History. I believe that it was Robin (R.G.D.) Laffan, director of studies in History at Queens', who introduced us. Robin was a Life Fellow and had been a major figure in the college for many years, though this is not apparent from some somewhat snide references to him in the college history by John Twigg, which appear to be based on one student's diary. (Elsewhere in the book, however, Twigg does refer to Laffan in a more positive way.) Robin Laffan was a gifted linguist, having, I think, learned Serbo-Croat during the First War, when he served as an army chaplain in the Balkans. He also spoke German very well, though with such a strong Austrian accent that on one occasion he was refused entrance to a pension in Munich, the landlady declaring 'We want no Austrians here.' In the 1940s undergraduates at Queens' were fascinated by the procession of Orthodox priests who came to Cambridge to Visit Robin. His international contacts enabled him to assist Walter Ullmann – who, as a judge, had had no hesitation in sentencing Nazi hooligans – when this young Austrian, barely escaped from Vienna at the Anschluss, arrived in England with no money (and virtually no English).

In 1949 it was Robin who sent me to Ullmann, by then established in Cambridge though still far distant from the chair which was eventually to be created for him at Trinity in Medieval Intellectual History. I must admit that I did not profit as much as I should have done from this introduction. To a shy undergraduate of eighteen Ullmann could be terrifying and I did not enjoy reading my amateurish essays on medieval universities to someone familiar with every detail of legal history. The point, however, is that Laffan was trying to help a then unknown foreign scholar while paying me the compliment of directing me to someone he knew to be a great authority in the subject.

Robin Laffan must have known Alfred Gilbey for many years. Laffan had been Anglican chaplain at Queens' and a member of the High Anglican Oratory of the Good Shepherd. His conversion to Catholicism in 1933 created a sensation. At that time Queens' was a small college, with only fourteen Fellows and a strong Low Church tradition. Laffan offered to resign and it was seriously proposed that his resignation should be accepted. Only the reaction of the leading scholar at Queens' at the time, Professor A. B. Cook, prevented this happening. Cook (himself a nonconformist) was able to insist that Laffan's outstanding services to the college should not be so easily forgotten. He is said to have stated that if Robin's resignation was accepted, he would himself resign and publish his reasons for doing so.

I have chosen to approach Alfred Gilbey by way of Robin Laffan, not only because it was through Robin that I came to know Alfred, but because the episode I have referred to illustrates the mental climate of Cambridge in the period before, and indeed in the decades immediately after, the Second World War. This was a time when Anglicanism was far more dominant than it is today and Catholicism was always viewed with suspicion, if not downright hostility. Throughout his life Alfred Gilbey was conscious that, as he put it, 'England is a Protestant country'. The fact that he was so extraordinarily successful in becoming part of the university world at Cambridge was due to his ability to understand and enter into the minds of others, Protestants as much as Catholics. He shared this ability with another of his friends, Outram Evennett, a fellow of Alfred's college, Trinity, and a distinguished historian of the sixteenth century. It was with another historian, Brian Wormald of Peterhouse (then an Anglican), that Alfred founded, in 1939, a Cambridge dining club, the Strafford, in memory of Charles I's minister Thomas Wentworth. At the dinners of the club Strafford's own prayer book and Roman Missal, occupying places of honour, symbolise the attempt in Charles's reign to reach a degree of understanding between the Churches of Rome and England.

I was fortunate enough to be elected to the Strafford Club in 1949 and, although teaching in North America largely removed me from England for several decades, I can recall many agreeable dinners in Cambridge – and later in London, at the Travellers' Club – with such friends as Dick Ladborough of Magdalene. Memories of June evenings at Childerley near Cambridge, when the club met to commemorate Charles I's visit to the house, are especially vivid. A passage from a contemporary account and another from that quintessential Cambridge figure, Arthur Benson, were always read aloud by Alfred himself, as the shadows gathered on the lawns of the house.

Alfred's unique social gifts were heavily stressed in his obituaries, almost to the exclusion, it seemed to me, of his religion. While there is no doubt that these gifts contributed greatly to the ease with which he moved in many different circles, in Cambridge and London, it was his faith that gave him the strength to survive the trials he endured during the turbulent decade of the 1960s, one which saw his departure, after thirty years as Catholic chaplain, from Fisher House, an institution which owed its survival entirely to him and where he chose to be buried.

We Believe, the book based on the instruction he gave to many undergraduates at Cambridge and later to many others in London, has been addressed already in this volume. While hewing closely to the lines of the Catechism, it contains many (extremely apposite) quotations that are unlikely to have occurred to anyone else, from half-forgotten authors such as W. H. Mallock, Montgomery Carmichael and Sheila Kaye-Smith, as well as references to buildings – Ely Cathedral, King's College Chapel – which he knew and loved. When I read the book I can hear Alfred's voice in the Great Chamber of Fisher House.

His *Commonplace Book* could only have been compiled by him. Here we have a number of aspects of his life, his appreciation of fox-hunting (which, for him, had to be expressed by his membership of the Trinity Foot Beagles), his love of Cambridge itself, his fondness for good company, and his general concept of society as one of degree and ordered hierarchy, evident by his placing first in the book the great speech from *Troilus and Cressida,* 'Take but degree away ...' Glancing through the list of authors who appear in the *Commonplace Book,* from Shakespeare to Maurice Baring, passing by Saintsbury, Santayana, J. H. Shorthouse, Belloc, and Arthur Machen (who seems to have contributed more extracts than anyone else), it seems to me that they illustrate very clearly not only Alfred's tastes but one of his principal strengths, his total indifference to literary – and other – fashions.

It would probably be impossible for any one writer to convey a picture of Alfred to those who did not know him. This is doubly the case because, since he died at the age of ninety-seven, he was predeceased by nearly all those who had known him when he was young. Apart from his Cambridge contemporaries who could have written about him, I regret the absence of his brilliant Oxford friends, such as Ronald Knox and David and Gervase Mathew, whom I recall seeing with him at Fisher House. The absence of their testimonies and those of many others whom I did not know personally is bound to lead to a somewhat one-sided picture. I am myself privileged to have seen Alfred in a number of different settings, not only at Fisher House but in the recreation of the Great Chamber there in his nephew's house at Rose Hill, and also in Spain, where he twice visited us in Majorca, celebrating the Tridentine Mass in our family chapel to the great pleasure of the congregation of farmers to whom it brought back memories of many years of an ancient liturgy happily devoid of the now obligatory sermon. It was also in Majorca that Alfred easily overcame any doubts our local priest might have had about permitting first communions in our chapel by remarking casually that he had himself received all the sacraments, including his ordination as a priest, in his own family's chapel. Other friends remember him at Jerez de la Frontera, when he came out from England to marry members of his mother's family. While he used to declare that he had only 'kitchen Spanish', he was in fact as much at home in Spain as in England, and his double inheritance, Spanish as well as English, goes some way to explain his many-sided gifts.

Alfred had the unusual gift of making anyone he met feel that he was interested in him. In the end what one most remembers is the extraordinary combination of seriousness and light-heartedness which underlay the sense of proportion one always sensed in Alfred. Within a year of his death, as he was getting into a taxi to return to the Travellers', he said to me, 'Now you're back in London, we can grow old together.'

Stephen Lambert

On 6 December 1996, at midday, in the Little Oratory, Monsignor Gilbey received an ex-Anglican into the Catholic Church. It was to be the last convert whom he had instructed; the last of a very long line that stretched back over more than sixty years of priesthood. The ceremony was dignified and, for the recipient, moving, for it came as the conclusion to forty-seven years spent in the Anglican communion, five of them as a priest. Not entirely unexpectedly, the solemnity of the occasion was leavened by the sort of minor drama that more than occasionally attended Alfred. The Holy Oil had been forgotten! The scene is easily imagined: a few moments of silent immobility before Alfred, already on fresh territory as the Service of Reception is being conducted in the vernacular rather than in Latin, looks expectantly at the Provost. The Provost returns the wordless question. After more silent moments slip by, the awful truth sinks in. The Provost departs in search of the vital ingredient as rapidly as liturgical decorum permits, leaving the Monsignor swaying a little unsteadily over his subject as the delay lengthens. The Faithful in the stalls, a little distracted from their devotions, wonder who is going to receive whom.

My instruction had been thorough and entirely 'by the book'. The book being, of course, *We Believe*, Alfred's timeless commentary on the Penny Catechism based on recordings of a course of instruction which he originally gave on a week by week basis. My instruction had to be fitted in with Alfred's busy diary and my trips to London, so it took most of a year. No 'law' was given on account of his age, or my situation as an Anglican priest in the Anglo-Catholic tradition. We worked through every page. We always met at the Travellers' Club in Pall Mall. Initially we began at 11 a.m.

and finished with lunch, but as anyone who has 'shared' a bottle of claret with Alfred will confirm, in his discipline and generosity he would toy with a glass and you end up drinking the rest! And so, in deference to the increasing tightness of my suits, late afternoon seemed a wiser time to foregather. His teaching and help over this period I will never forget, and although best known for his pre-Vatican II orthodoxy, Alfred was always able to speak authoritatively about current issues without seeming to be from another age. I suspect that this was because he said his prayers, and so what he taught lived in him.

No one who attended Mass within Alfred's 'chapel' (broom cupboard) in the Travellers' can forget the experience. The vestment cupboard took up a large portion of the available space: Alfred would vest and, biretta in place, tread his clerical shuffle the distance of some six feet to the altar. More often than not I seemed to pick a hot summer evening to attend and the heat in that small place of devotion was indescribable.

The *Daily Telegraph* obituary of Alfred Gilbey very properly recorded his devotion to the Trinity Foot Beagles. I was, at first, somewhat surprised by this loyalty because I imagined that such an ordered and immaculate person would have found the fenland plough too dreadful to contemplate, especially for the ghastly effect it has on clothing. How wrong I was. Alfred not only adored his days on the fens but also emerged at the end of the day with hardly a speck of mud on that wonderful cleric suiting in which he hunted. Although he had retired from the chaplaincy two years before I arrived at Cambridge, the Monsignor travelled up from London to beagle on many Saturdays. Always surrounded in the field by young men who quickly fell under his spell, he entertained and broadened the minds of numerous undergraduates by his conversation and by his remarkable knowledge of who was related to whom, and how they fitted into the history of this or that house (usually an architectural gem and often the seat of a famous recusant family in the bad days that followed the Reformation).

Those who grew to know him and love him often found themselves privileged to be guests or even members of the Strafford

Club, a dining club founded in the memory of Thomas Wentworth, 1st Earl of Strafford. The club met (as it still does) once a term, always on a major feast day, often St Andrew's Day in the Michaelmas term and Candlemass Day in the Lent term. Here sherry was offered before dinner and claret during the meal. *Never port*. The highlight of the evening was the after dinner speech, almost always by a speaker of exceptional quality and knowledge, often without a note. In the summer term the club paid a visit to Childerley Hall, for the 'Childerley picnic'. Many beaglers became members of the Strafford Club and were perhaps more educated by these evenings than by their tutors. After such a dinner at Trinity one Saturday night, I walked down King's Parade with Alfred, and a young man of the town, whose capacity for beer was less than his thirst, swept off the Monsignor's clerical hat and bowled it like a tyre along the street. Alfred did not hesitate in his conversation. Order was restored when a colleague of mine retrieved the hat. Alfred simply interspersed a murmured 'Thank you' into the dialogue.

He missed the annual visit of the Trinity Foot Beagles to Northumberland only once, as far as I know. This occurred owing to the sorry fact of the sale of The Three Wheatheads in Thropton late in 1995, when the landlady of many years standing retired. Her departure caught Alfred out. Accustomed always to telephoning the inn about ten days in advance of taking up residence, and finding that he had been long expected, he telephoned in August 1996 expecting the usual courteous welcome. But the manager had never heard of the Monsignor. And the room had been let many weeks ago. Alfred took the news, as always, with complete acceptance, telling me: 'Alas, I shall not be with you this year. I telephoned The Three Wheatheads to take my accustomed room, only to be met with disappointment.' Master of understatement.

On Saturday 27 September 1997 the Monsignor had his final Northumberland day with the TFB. I had asked him to bless the hounds at the meet, for we had suspected that it would not be long before he would be leaving this world. As happened from time to time, Alfred was awfully late. I had nearly given up hope of his arriving and was about to move off when Nicholas Lorriman's car was spied with the dark figure bent within the passenger's seat. 'I am most awfully sorry to have kept you. I suffered a poor night's sleep, almost certainly due to my excitement at coming beagling, and I dropped off just when I should have been getting up. And in my enthusiasm to come North, I failed to pack my breeches, so you find me, alas, improperly dressed.'

His last day at Cambridge was on a very cold day during the winter of 1997/98 when the hounds were hunting near Cottenham. Philip Bonn drove him and he followed all day in the car. I marvelled that he combined the beagling with the serious study of some learned publication with which David Watkin had sent him out. I saw him give both the hunting and the book great attention. (I am not sure which gave the greater benefit!) He had tea with us in an inn at Cottenham and I felt certain that the Monsignor's days with the TFB were now over.

Alfred was much more than the proverbial 'character'. He had immense influence for good on so many people's lives and the teaching that he passed on has made the world an infinitely better – and much funnier – place.

Hugh-Guy Lorriman

I was sitting in my office in March 1998 (I was twenty-three) when Paul Doyle, a great friend of David Watkin and of Monsignor Gilbey, telephoned to give me the news that the Monsignor had died. I replaced the receiver and – it is the one time I have been given this gift on hearing of the death of a loved one – I wept.

As a child My brothers and I knew the Monsignor from the earliest age for two reasons: his intimate friendship with my father and because he was godfather to my eldest brother, Gregory. I remember, going back to the age of seven, sitting in the splendour of the coffee room at the Travellers' for lunch. It would be the first day back from prep school and our party was composed of my father, my two brothers, and our host, Monsignor Gilbey – always at the customary corner table. Afterwards we would sit in the library or smoking-room and I would write letters with the dip pen. Monsignor Gilbey much admired and encouraged my epistolary enthusiasm. These were magical moments in my childhood. I was always struck by his kindness, the aura of holiness that surrounded him. As little children we were welcomed with our father to come into the Monsignor's most personal environment, his room at the Travellers' Club, with the pictures of Cambridge and the Pear's soap in the basin.

I was always aware of Monsignor's Gilbey's love for my father. One of his traits, perhaps a product of his Spanish blood, was a complete openness of heart. He carried with him everywhere a small leather photo-case with two photos of my father, one in Trinity Foot Beagles uniform and the other of him holding a beagle puppy at the kennels (from Papa's Cambridge days). He used often to say to me 'I worship your father' in that open way so characteristic of him. I used to feel this to be a deep bond between us.

In his last years he came down to our home in Kent to spend Christmas with us, a great blessing. We were able to hear Mass for a week in the simple beauty of the Tridentine rite. As a Latin scholar I was even privileged to serve his Mass once or twice. I remember a hilarious moment when Monsignor Gilbey was offering daily Mass for the parish. The small local congregation, rather amazed at finding all in Latin, approached to receive communion. Some came forward hands outstretched, as has become common custom. The celebrant was having none of it. He very deliberately targeted the parishioners' mouths. I almost laughed aloud as I watched the somewhat bewildered faces forced to open their mouths to receive the Blessed Sacrament on the tongue.

As a young man As a young man, the person and friendship of Monsignor Gilbey were of inestimable importance to me. It was his integrity which conveyed itself so strongly. This combined with his loving heart made him an irresistible figure for myself and for so many others of my generation. His complete confidence and seren- ity communicated itself almost miraculously to those whose lives he touched.

He was a holy man. He trusted totally in the salvation worked by Our Blessed Lord. It was that salvation which mattered, not our own endeavours. So, confident in salvation achieved, Monsignor Gilbey loved Our Lord's creation and embraced that creation. This, it seems to me, was why he was so able to love and be loved. His trust in providence was the foundation of his remarkable ease, con- fidence and charm.

Only now can I see how perfectly he lived out his life, accepting what God had given him and loving it. He loved his Latin roots and his beloved England (at the end of seven o'clock rosary he always added an extra Hail Mary with the introduction: 'Jesus convert England, Jesus have mercy on this country'). He loved the Trav- ellers' Club, he loved hunting, he loved the traditional vestments that proclaimed his sacramental ministry and beautified his person, God's creation. He was completely himself, and served his Saviour through these things. To hunt in finest beagling attire became an act of divine worship.

Who made you? There were two statements, insistently repeated by him, which seem to me to sum up his life and message.

The first took the form of questions 1 and 2 of the Penny Catechism:

> Who made you?
> *God made you.*
> Why did he make you?
> *To know him, love him and serve him in this world and be happy with him forever in the next.*

The second was: 'There is always time for the sacraments'.

How many times I heard him say these two things, expecting the words and rejoicing to hear them. When I first heard him repeat those two questions from the Catechism, so pointedly avoiding any polemical gloss, I could not help thinking – 'How can one say that to an agnostic world?' Yet repeating the simple truth is often most helpful to oneself and others: let the truth speak for itself. 'Who made you? *God made you.*' Monsignor Gilbey urged us in his words and actions to accept that God made us perfectly for Him, therefore we must accept what we are, love what we are, and indeed positively enjoy ourselves. Second, he proclaimed that God gives us the sacraments – God's special gift of grace to us. His friendship constituted an invitation to those sacraments and his sacramental mission was the driving force of his grace-filled life.

I recall how, when I had the privilege of dining with Monsignor Gilbey in the Travellers', at the end of the meal I would often ask, with some diffidence, whether he might have time to hear my confession. I always knew the response. Pause – 'There is always time for the sacraments.' I heard it with joy in my heart. I have a great love for the sacrament of confession. I am sure that Our Lord worked to give me this gift especially through the ministry of Monsignor Gilbey. I cannot remember without emotion sitting close to him and hearing the kind words of his quiet voice punctuated with characteristic pauses and sudden bursts of advice. How wonderful that ministry was for me, dating from childhood to my days as a working man.

Monsignor Gilbey loved the deep mysteries of the faith. He often said to me, quoting the Gloria, that one must praise God (very slowly) 'FOR HIS GREAT GLORY – PER MAGNAM GLORIAM TUAM.' Perhaps one of the greatest things he taught me was a simple openness to truth before intellectual explorations. PER MAGNAM GLORIAM TUAM. His priority was not to explain. He proclaimed. It is wonderful.

Sitting and talking with Monsignor Gilbey Monsignor Gilbey's person and his holiness attracted the younger generation. When I organised a play in the summer of 1997 which was rehearsed and performed over a week, the Monsignor was visiting us and would take his meals with the family and all the young people involved. I remember afterwards asking one of the young actresses who was playing Cecily (*The Importance of Being Earnest)* what she most enjoyed about the week. I was perhaps hoping for some recognition of my own efforts in reference to the play. In response she said, with sheer delight in her voice, that what she most enjoyed was sitting and talking with Monsignor Gilbey.

In terms of his age, I was always amused at the difference of perception between the older and younger generations. My father's generation had known Monsignor Gilbey in his vigorous Cambridge days. In his latter years I would hear them say such phrases as 'Alfred is looking so frail.' Charles des Forges and I used to laugh at this. To us he never looked any different, no older than when I was seven years old. He was such a constant figure, of such simple integrity, that he never changed, even physically. His death came as a considerable shock. I had never seriously thought of him leaving us.

Hope At times I long for Monsignor Gilbey's presence, that wonderful integrity centred in the confident pursuit of holiness – as an Englishman, with a Spanish mother, a lover of wine, of hunting and of elegance, a lover of family and degree, a Catholic priest wholly devoted to the sacraments. I found this all so comforting.

But I live in hope, the hope of our glorious Faith. Since Monsignor Gilbey's death the truths he presented and lived out seem ever more vivid. I know that he is praying for me and rejoicing when I receive the sacraments, and loving my father more than ever, perfectly in fact. His example and his friendship are, I know, truly alive and accompany me every day.

PER MAGNAM GLORIAM TUAM

Nicholas Lorriman

For those privileged enough to have been familiar with his conversation, none could doubt that Alfred had a *bête noire*: egalitarianism. It was for him the root disorder in Church and State, and in society in general. There is a sense in which Alfred's most vibrant inspiration was his desire to propagate and exemplify the counter principle: the necessity of hierarchy. This was to oppose the degrading tendencies at work since the fall of man in general, and, in a more local perspective, since that cataclysmic exaltation of unregenerate man, the French Revolution. He was wont to refer to 'the infinite and merciful gradations of a hierarchical society'. Alfred was a traditionalist in the fundamental sense of believing that life cannot be led otherwise than in conformity to nature: things as they are. Things are naturally hierarchical. He knew the utopian vision of self-perfecting human nature to be self-defeating, ending in frustration and the death-wish. Hierarchy is the condition of life. One experienced his extraordinary, almost exuberant, vitality as a living confirmation of his philosophy. It was also a keynote of his fascination. He knew that true seriousness – and nobody could have been more profoundly serious – was inseparable from gaiety. He would have said that one of the most serious things about life is the necessity to *make* happiness. Alfred liked to remind us that 'happiness is an artefact'. Alfred's gift of irony, never unkind and often directed at himself, hinged much on this paradox, as in his assertion, particularly after his move from Cambridge to London, 'I am now living entirely for pleasure'. And why did Alfred attract such love and devotion? Surely, because of his unique ability to give pleasure and communicate happiness. Alfred made so many people happy – and of course in the deeper sense of restoring confidence, helping those suffering from the peculiarly modern scourge of insecurity, even loss of identity, to find themselves again.

To be a member of Alfred's last generation of undergraduates was to be aware – and the more acutely with hindsight – of all that he had done to create a haven of traditional values at Fisher House. So many of us came up to Cambridge, from every sort of background, instinctively aspiring to the civilising influences of an ancient university. We gravitated towards Fisher House because there we found a microcosm of so much one had dreamt Cambridge would be. Fisher House could offer what so many colleges were increasingly ceasing to offer, a gracious and humane setting for study, social exchange, and the practice of religion. On the scale, as it were, of a doll's house in comparison with the grander colleges, Alfred's Fisher House captured much of the atmosphere of the ideal college: the enchanting miniature court-yard with its fig-tree and Della Robbia medallion of Madonna and Child enclosed by opposing two-storey wings, these linked together by the chaplain's house. One wing was composed, with a touch of eccentricity, of superimposed chapels. The ground floor of the other wing was the book-lined Fisher Room, with grand piano, stage and columned proscenium arch, used for such activities as Fisher Society meetings, the Dominican lectures, the Fisher Revue, and Alfred's Sunday afternoon tea-parties. On the first floor was the library, with its well-stocked shelves, reading tables and lamps, leather armchairs and settles, and portraits: all much in the style of a club library. The chaplain's house was elegant and intimate but with a touch of grandness (the Great Chamber and the Bishop's Room) – something of what one might expect of a Master's Lodge.

But for the pious Catholic undergraduate or for the inquiring Anglican, there could be no doubt that within this gracious setting Alfred's central inspiration was providing an anchor of Catholic life for his undergraduate flock. Alfred's priestly zeal was the animating principle of Fisher House. He dispensed the sacraments and gave spiritual instruction and comfort with a tireless availability which had echoes of the style and energy of his priestly hero Robert Hugh

Benson (1871–1914) who, he used to say, had influenced him more in deciding his vocation than anyone he *never* knew. There was a constant stream of visitors from after the daily 7.30 a.m. Mass to well beyond the dinner hour, often beyond midnight. One of the most familiar sights at Fisher House was Alfred's smiling open-armed welcome, accompanied by the phrase 'Come right in'. And when one came in, one would be the beneficiary of Alfred's double *modus operandi*, a person to person exchange, where one felt one was Alfred's entire focus of interest, and a warm social atmosphere, where Alfred exercised his gifts for bringing people together: 'I like my friends to like each other.'

Alfred was, one might say, obsessed with the unique importance of the human person. He was haunted by the thought that everything else would pass, but that each person who ever crossed one's path was going on for ever and ever. His radical anti-egalitarianism was built on the knowledge that the whole redemptive act could only benefit individual souls, not any collectivity. He radiated fraternal charity because he saw the immortal soul in everyone he came in contact with, just as one felt, when he raised the Host at the *'Ecce Agnus Dei'* at the people's communion, that he 'saw' his Lord in glory. Hence his delight in bringing people together and being a catalyst for ring upon ring of friendships; hence his attentiveness to the individual, so that so many people felt they had a special place in his affections – how clearly this appeared at his death. Paradoxically, especially in the light of so many having a sense of an exclusive link, there is a sense in which Alfred's approach to personal relations was marked by self-effacement. He was very conscious of the responsibilities corresponding to one's gifts. His abundant gifts of charm were very clearly for him, particularly in his priestly character, a means to draw people to the Lord. His friendship carried with it a permanent, implicit invitation to the sacraments. For someone needing the comfort of Holy Communion and unable to attend Mass, he would happily, in a mode now out of favour, give communion from the tabernacle. Confession was available literally at any time. In one critical moment, Alfred absolved me under an archway in a busy London street. A scrupulous friend requesting confession but fearful of imposing on Alfred's time was met with the response 'There is always time for the sacraments'.

Alfred's central preoccupation with the uniqueness of the individual was reflected in his own highly individual style. His integrity, his wholeness, the sense of which was a comfort to so many, sprang from a fundamental truth to himself. He knew exactly who he was, what he believed in and what he liked. He had an immediate apprehension of God's creative love for him, and this gave him a self-confidence which was the contrary of self-satisfaction. It was the self-confidence that is the condition of self-giving, in line with the scriptural principle that properly ordered love of self is the necessary condition of altruism, the ordering of that love being the radical primacy of the relationship with God. Alfred referred to the necessity of getting the 'vertical' relationship with God right before we could hope to succeed in 'horizontal' relationships with others. Alfred was deeply grateful for the grace that he shared with Cardinal Newman of an immediate sense of his Creator. He liked to quote Newman as one who could never remember a time when he was not aware of 'two, and two only, luminous and self-evident beings, myself and Almighty God'.

Alfred's view of education was necessarily 'vertical' and hierarchical, the duty of the educator being to draw those in his charge up towards the highest values, not degrade them to some socially engineered common denominator. The majority of undergraduates coming to the Chaplaincy responded positively to this approach. Alfred's approach was nothing if not inclusive. This was not just because of his warm temperament and attraction to people but because his was an inclusive philosophy. If you are all looking up toward higher things, you can all look together whatever your point of departure may be; on the contrary, the egalitarian or lowest common denominator approach must necessarily exclude everything that is not itself. Alfred liked the analogy of the bowl of sugar: you can't level upwards, only downwards. Anybody who really knew Alfred's chaplaincy would know that it attracted undergraduates from a wide variety of educational and social backgrounds. It was precisely those from so-called less privileged backgrounds who often drew particular comfort and inspiration from the higher things that Alfred cultivated with such style, warmth, and generosity. Obviously, it would not be possible to enjoy such an atmosphere if you were actively hostile to the philosophy behind it. It is significant that those who did, in the iconoclastic atmosphere of the '60s, challenge Alfred's stance indulged remarkably little in the sort of tendentious caricature to which his aristocratically idiosyncratic figure could so easily have lent itself.

Central to Alfred's religious vision was his belief in Divine Providence. He felt immense gratitude to God for the providential design of his own life, particularly concerning the apparently negative moments which in fact turned out to have especially fulfilling consequences. This can be appreciated in the circumstances of his going up to Cambridge and of his finally leaving. His family would have liked him to go to Oxford, but the academic limitations of Beaumont meant that he had no Greek, a bar to Oxford but not to Cambridge. Alfred's leaving Cambridge was not a happy moment. The harsh winds of change that rose so brusquely in the '60s blew on Alfred in the form of undergraduate pressure groups and certain senior members belonging to the CUCA (Cambridge University Catholic Association) who made it clear that his pastoral policies and style were, in their view, no longer 'relevant to the times'. Alfred was an intense believer in the need to stand on principle, as his successful fight to save Fisher House from the developers had born witness, but not in matters inessential (i.e. matters not concerning faith or morals), if confrontation were in danger of being unedifying or ineffective: Alfred deplored the exercise of 'ineffective sanctions'. The authority (the Oxford and Cambridge Catholic Education Board) that had appointed him was not likely to be behind him, and there was in the meantime the prospect of an ongoing conflict between himself and a vocal minority of undergraduates now controlling the Fisher Society, along with certain 'forward-looking' senior members. Both groups were pressing for a more 'democratic' chaplaincy, with student representation in its running and the integration of women.

Alfred avoided collision by offering his retirement a year earlier than he had intended. He thus avoided an acrimonious conclusion to his long tenure and spared his opponents exposure to accusations of gross ingratitude after one hundred terms of devoted, generous, and markedly successful (a term Alfred would not have liked) service. One thinks of the exceptional number of converts he had instructed and received, and the many vocations to the priesthood of old members of his Cambridge flock. This was an occasion that demonstrated Alfred's capacity to practise his counsel of detachment from considerations of failure or hurt feelings. 'Bonum est mihi quia humiliasti me' was a favourite verse from the Psalter. One of his striking formulas concerning the need for detachment was 'Never give anyone the power to hurt you', meaning, never let your self-esteem depend on what others do to you, or may think of you. 'What will it matter in a hundred years' time?' He had a particular horror of the affliction of 'the chip on the shoulder'. As he pointed out, nobody can take it off but the sufferer, he being the least inclined to do so. Alfred possessed entirely a quality he so much admired in others: lack of self-pity. He went from Cambridge serenely and without recrimination.

He did nevertheless have a practical problem: he had nowhere to go. It was then that he saw the solution to his temporary homelessness in taking up his abode at the Travellers' as so wonderfully providential. He had considered a flat in Cambridge. There was also a serious suggestion that he might take on the chaplaincy to the Household Division. This would have given him an official job and agreeable quarters in Wellington Barracks. His hesitations about the first option focused on the risk of finding himself without a clear role and on the fringe of a world where he had been so central. The second option, though giving him a role, represented a break in continuity which he felt he might find difficult to handle: being uprooted from the university world whose atmosphere and structures he loved and knew intimately, he would find himself plunged into a military milieu with which he had only the most tenuous connections. In this period of instability, he, to use his own phrase, 'lived in a suitcase'. On leaving Cambridge he initially stayed at the

Athenaeum. To meet the problem of a member not being able to exceed ten days of continuous residence in the club he joined the Travellers', and for a period of two or three months 'commuted' with his suitcases between the two clubs, as the permitted period at each expired. In those happier days when club rules were less rigidly institutionalised and when a club Secretary, himself a member, could feel free to show flexibility when particular needs were involved, Alfred fell on, as it were, almost accidentally, the solution to his homelessness that was to prove so happily providential for the next thirty-two years of his life. The club Secretary suggested he prolong his residence indefinitely at the Travellers'.

It is possible to feel that the London life he established in the particular setting of the Travellers' was if anything more congenial to his genius and special calling than his Cambridge life. His genius was his ability to embody, in his style and mode of being, the values he loved, so making them lovable to others. He summarised his special calling as being his abiding desire 'to recommend the religion he loved to the country he loved'. At the Travellers' he was entirely integrated into an eminently English institution, whereas at Cambridge he could not but remain to a degree peripheral to college and academic life. It was not just club life that suited him, but just that expression of it exemplified at the Travellers'. Alfred liked to point out that Barry's building of 1830 had a Regency elegance and lightness contrasting with the more ponderous Victorian note struck by the adjoining club, the Reform, built only ten years later but already echoing Victorian earnestness. Alfred had a sense of the particularity of place running parallel to his sense of the uniqueness of the individual. The Travellers' was just right for him, just as he felt Pall Mall to be the ideal London location. When asked whether he enjoyed living in London, he would suggest the vacuity of the question by saying that if one meant did he like living in the square mile bordered by St James's Park and Piccadilly, his answer was 'Yes, very much indeed!'

The period at the Travellers' was not a static one of retirement, but one where his personal impact grew to fullness; for wide circles of friends and admirers he effectively attained icon-status, seeming a living symbol of traditional values. And it really was Alfred personally embodying what he believed in and loved. He no longer had, as at Fisher House, a place which he could shape to express his values. His clerical style could no longer be seen as an echo of the established patterns of the Church; while in the context of the Travellers' Club, there seemed a harmony between his person and his elegant setting that underlined his personifying those traditional club values which many members seemed increasingly ready to abandon.

The club was Alfred's home in the sense that he lived there continuously, and enjoyed that freedom of use that is the privilege of membership. His use of the club was in a way a reflection of a key aspect of his personality: an irrepressible outward flow of energy, balanced and controlled by inner serenity and peace. Alfred was in constant movement between the club rooms while engaging in quasi-permanent conversation: in the coffee-room and smoking-room with his innumerable guests; in the Morning Room, if he was entertaining a lady; in the recess off the Hall where he found seclusion suitable to giving instructions in the Faith, or hearing the occasional confession – a continuum of personal exchange sustained by greetings from members, or, as often, from the guests of members by whom he would be enthusiastically recognised. The library was a place where in the rare moments he had to himself he could quietly consult a volume or read *The Times*, as one published photograph shows him elegantly so doing, though the picture of him there that comes most spontaneously to mind is rather of him, book in hand, moving to or from the shelves, as likely as not looking up a reference to give to a friend.

Alfred's two privileges – a permanent bedroom and his own chapel – were the focus points of the stillness at the centre ('Be still and know that I am God' was a verse from the Psalter he specially loved), the intimation of which communicated a sense of peace to so many friends and admirers. Those fortunate friends who went to room 9 will remember the three abrupt steps up to the L-shaped corridor, with only two other rooms on it. There was a homely elegance about the room that gave it an emotional tone especially

Alfred's. The pictures were a summary of his loves and roots: the Roman prints over the head of the bed, with a print of the London Pantheon – once his family firm's offices – echoing the Roman original alongside; on the opposite wall, prints of Trinity; by the door, a print of Beaumont; by the wash basin, a watercolour of his home Mark Hall by Basil Johnson, the friend who, from his adolescence, had been a key influence on his interests and tastes. On the wash basin there was the amber bar of Pear's soap that he carefully shaped into a translucent dome (the technique being to take the convex remnant of the preceding bar and insert it into the concavity of the new bar, then being careful to rub the grafted bar between the hands in a circular, rather than horizontal, movement). One remembers Alfred's ivory toilet set, the tin of Coty Chypre talc, and the assorted lotions from Truefitt and Hill, disposed in immaculate order on the dressing-table; behind the door would hang the spotted silk dressing-gown and the red-piped cassock – one recalls glimpses of Alfred doing up the innumerable red buttons before putting on his buckled 'party shoes'. Another familiar sight was Alfred sitting on the red coverlet of the bed initiating, or more likely, receiving a call on the bedside telephone. A leather club armchair, squeezed between the foot of the bed and the chest-of-drawers, was a pivotal feature. Perhaps the most abiding image of that room is of coming in at the door and seeing Alfred facing you in the armchair, the Roman breviary in his hands, spectacles on nose, lips moving. It was a peaceful room. Perhaps nothing spoke to me more of the intrinsic harmony of Alfred's life than his gift of sound sleep. 'Did you sleep well, Alfred?'; 'Like a child.' I saw him settling in bed for sleep, pulling the medal of Our Lady of Perpetual Succour from the neck of his nightshirt to kiss it before turning on his side with his rosary twined around his fingers, then, in old age, his face in profile seeming as delicate and peaceful as a child's.

Alfred's life constantly exemplified his conviction that the present moment was just the right one for those trying to do the will of Almighty God and that it was mistaken to imagine oneself better off in periods of history other than one's own. At what other moment in an age of religious indifferentism, with the English protestant spirit unassertive, and when a well-disposed member Secretary still had power in the club, could a Roman Catholic priest have hoped to have been allowed to keep a private chapel in an English gentlemen's club? Alfred's happy establishment in the club owed so much to Robin McDouall, the Secretary at the time of Alfred's joining. It was also he who suggested that Alfred might like to install a chapel in the retired valet Jock's so-called 'music room' – Alfred conjectured that Jock must have listened to the wireless there. It was a diminutive attic room at the top of a precipitous back-staircase serving the service wing.

Alfred's serenity was certainly the product of an ordered and prayerful life, but even more of his central quality, a loving heart. People were so strongly drawn to him because his presence was serene and loving. To lose the traditional Catholic devotion to the Blessed Sacrament, as we seem in danger of doing now, would certainly be to lose the sort of effects so clear in Alfred. His loving heart was nurtured by his intimacy with Our Lord, present in the Blessed Sacrament. His immediate sense of the Real Presence and his worship of that Presence was his central devotion. The intimacy of the tiny chapel symbolised that relationship. The rich materials and mellow colours radiated warmth: the damask altar hangings, the pale-gold tabernacle veil with the motif of the hart enchained, the green wallpaper and the pale-green silk, eighteenth-century, flowered Roman chasuble; then, the wooden furnishings: the dark mahogany vesting chest, the relic cases, the prie-Dieu, the walnut glow of the richly carved William and Mary armchair, the finely turned wooden altar-lectern. There were three representations of the human person: the tender icon of Our Lady of Perpetual Succour, with its rich, gold ground; the sensitive melancholy of the Holbein drawing of St John Fisher; and centrally, the slender ivory figure of Our Lord above the altar, with its framed cross surmounted by a light rococo flourish of gold branch-work. Most poignantly there hung to the right of the altar a framed obituary card of Antonia, Alfred's beloved nurse who had accompanied him in her old age to Fisher House (his mother had remembered first seeing her, a peasant girl, walking down from the hills above Jerez, with jasmine in her hair). So much humanity in a room that seemed, to use Alfred's phrase, 'no bigger than a cigar box'.

The intimacy of the chapel fitted well with it having an especially personal status in his London ministry. His regular daily Mass was a 'public' one (in the sense of being open to the public though not publicly announced, this not being permissible for a Tridentine Mass) celebrated at Our Lady of the Assumption, Warwick Street in an earlier period, and subsequently in St Wilfrid's chapel at the Brompton Oratory. The Travellers' chapel, above all, ensured that Alfred had the Reserved Sacrament, so to speak, under his own roof; it was also a convenience which enabled him to celebrate Mass at times when a public altar was not easily available: on Sundays, or on returning from a journey, for example. On such occasions he would ask a friend to serve him. Preparing for Mass, one remembers Alfred gingerly stepping down the precipitous staircase with Mrs Glockner's (his housekeeper for twenty years at Fisher House) cruets precariously poised on their glass tray on his way to his room to fill them with wine and water; or he might have asked his server to take care of the 'recruits' (a reference to a Spanish Franciscan lay-brother's version of the word). Many of us remember that wonderful intimacy, incompatible with the spirit and form of the new rite, of priest and server. The sense of recollection of the old Mass was enhanced in this confined setting. Alfred's presence was so vivid, the stooped figure in the Roman chasuble with at its top the protruding ridge of the white amice, the red-tasselled biretta, the gold chalice adorned with stones from his mother's rings, the horn-rimmed spectacles hunted for in the pocket of his cassock: all these personal traits absorbed into the dramatic flow of ritual gesture and the murmured rhythm of the sacred texts, the whole intensified by the loving concentration of the celebrant.

Alfred was of course always delighted to have a congregation, and two or three would often gather. The 6 p.m. Thursday evening Mass was the only celebration officially announced to interested members of the club. It drew a regular congregation: mainly Catholics but with a sprinkling of Anglicans for whom the old rite was one of the attractions of the Faith. On these occasions, as many

as ten men, being or seeming big, in contrast to Alfred's slight
figure, would be crammed into the chapel, pressed against the wall
or kneeling awkwardly on hassocks, turning the pages of their
Roman Missals in concentrated silence. There was something of
the feeling of a recusant remnant keeping the Faith, in opposition to
an indifferent world and, ironically, to an increasingly uncompre-
hending and even hostile Church.

The Thursday evening Mass was part of the way Alfred gave to
his London life a basic but sustaining structure. From his arrival in
London, the 'old boys' of his Cambridge flock were invited to a 6
p.m. Mass in the Lady Chapel at Farm Street, on every first Friday
of the month and on the immediately preceding Thursday. Alfred
was available to hear confessions during the hour before Mass.
After Mass, the congregation was invited to join him at a nearby
pub: for years The Running Footman. His scrupulous insistence on
always sending out a personalised invitation to the several hundred
'old boys' in his card-index represented the inside of two days'
work a month. He was particularly grateful when a friend would
sit with him (usually in the Committee Room), sharing the chore of
addressing, stamping and closing envelopes. He derived a certain
enjoyment from the conscientious performance of this monthly
task, as if it went in some way to compensate for his more general
incapacity in administrative matters.

The key to his daily rhythm was his systematically early rise at
5.45 a.m., giving him time to re-collect himself and be prepared to
leave the club before 7 a.m., in order to celebrate a 7.30 a.m. Mass.
For the latter, and longer, period of his London life this took place
in St Wilfrid's chapel at the London Oratory. These celebrations, as
those at Farm Street, increasingly drew members of his new
London flock, steadily building up as a complement to his Cambridge flock. Within this basic framework of pastoral commitment
(to which must be added his regular Sunday visits to his cousin
Walter Gilbey's house at Rose Hill, near Henley, where he celebrated Mass for Catholics of the locality), Alfred's time was filled
giving spiritual and social succour to members of his old and new
flocks. Hardly a week would go by when he could not be seen hur-

riedly descending the steps of the club carrying two heavy suitcases, about to hail a taxi, on his way to perform some sacramental ministry – christening, wedding, funeral, or anniversary Mass – for members of his double flock. In this way, Alfred was constantly radiating out from the Travellers', exercising his apostolate in many places, with particularly frequent returns to Cambridge. Here he kept up links with his many friends, with his old college, and with Fisher House, where, though clearly out of sympathy with the new order introduced there, he remained on the warmest terms with successive chaplains – Alfred's freedom to perform this, as it were, roving ministry answered many spiritual needs. As he pointed out, for a number of his friends, particularly those who had not been to Catholic schools, he was the only priest they knew. In a time of painful liturgical transition, he was also able to bring the traditional dignity of sacramental celebration, a dignity that more of the faithful than the Church can bring herself to admit craved, and still crave.

The club remained the springboard for all this activity. Alfred deliberately avoided getting involved in club politics, feeling that his privileged status disqualified him from appearing to exert influence on club policy. As exceptions to this approach, it may be mentioned that he did sit on the wine committee (appropriate and neutral ground) for a period; and, more significantly, he did play an active role in stopping the proposal that the recess off the Hall should be turned into a bar. There was a point at which motives of cost-effectiveness became incompatible with the identity of a gentlemen's club. 'A club', said Alfred, 'should be run as an amenity not as a business.' He suggested that the bold solution to concern about the club's viability would have been the determination to remain the only one amongst the big nineteenth-century clubs to retain its exclusively male character. Exclusiveness always being a good selling-point, Alfred reckoned people would have been queuing up to join. It was regrettable to him that the Travellers' authorities succumbed to the pressures of fashion and allowed the ladies a progressively greater use of the club.

The tactics employed to effect the policy introducing women

Alfred described as 'grandma's footsteps', two steps forward and one step back, the authorities always giving the impression that the latest concession would be the last. But as Alfred indicated in one of his luminous formulas, in this as in other graver contexts, 'Once you admit a false principle, there is no point at which you can arrest its consequences.' Alfred would have been well placed to organise a pressure group, had he been so inclined. There was a sizeable nucleus in the club closely sympathetic to his views. But Alfred eschewed confrontation, and though deploring the slide away from the traditional pattern of a gentlemen's club, remained throughout his tenure at the Travellers' profoundly grateful for the consideration and understanding he never failed to receive, as well from those presiding over the club's destinies as from its devoted staff. He certainly helped to stimulate membership, introducing a steady flow of new members, many, though by no means all, Catholics. He had been much amused by a conversation that had been overheard between two old members: 'There are a lot of Roman Catholics in this club' – pause – 'you hear 'em laughin' and talkin' together!' 'They have something to laugh and talk about' was Alfred's comment.

This happy condition of being a Catholic Alfred had heard alluded to in the following dismissive remark: 'Roman Catholics live in a fairyland of their own.' 'Yes,' commented Alfred, 'but it happens to be true.' He became increasingly impatient of the qualifying *terra*, with its suggestion of limitation. No, one was simply a Catholic belonging to the Catholic Church. He preferred to highlight the universality of the one, true Faith. He was there to remind us that being a Catholic implies not only a theology and a dogmatic position, but a whole philosophy of life. In our dualistic world where religion has been marginalised to become the preserve of clerics and minorities of enthusiasts, and philosophy has divorced itself from theology, Alfred's thought and mode of life had a liberating effect because they seemed a living demonstration that the Catholic 'fairyland' encompassed the whole of life, natural as well as supernatural. In a religious climate subtly but pervasively marked by puritan and Jansenist influences, it was a revelation to realise that cultivating the amenities and pleasures of civilisation and its higher achievements was a fulfilment of Catholicism and not just an accidental adjunct.

An important aspect of Alfred's impact was to help people find freedom from the tensions arising from certain uncomfortable dualities. There is always a potential conflict of loyalties for the English Catholic. Alfred highlighted this by suggesting that there was a book to be written contrasting those Catholics leaders of this century, like Paul Neville (monk of Ampleforth and Headmaster of Ampleforth College 1924–54) and Cardinal Hinsley, who had sought integration into the English achievement, with others, like Chesterton and Belloc, who had wanted to distance themselves from it. Alfred's exuberantly confident Catholicism with its Spanish background, happily combining with an uninhibited delight in the whole English tradition (expressed in his extraordinarily wide and detailed knowledge of English architecture, social history, and of the Church of England) seemed to resolve this dichotomy. This sense of reconciliation must have reassured the many Anglican men and women whose path to Rome included the experience of Alfred's conversation or formal instructions. And I feel sure I speak for many 'cradle' Catholics in saying that Alfred's example helped me to a new confidence in my identity as an English Catholic. Alfred's position was an eloquent reminder that Catholicism was catholic not only with the universality of Christian Revelation, but by taking up and perfecting within Revelation universal values that are to be found in any civilisation worthy of the name, and with a particular charm and sweetness in the traditional patterns of English life.

Another area where Alfred was a wonderful antidote to scruples was that concerning feelings of unease about, or frank rejection of, the *aggiornamento* initiated by the Second Vatican Council. There seemed almost a conspiracy putting pressure on one to believe that it was compulsory for any loyal Catholic to agree with the innovations coming out of Vatican II. It seemed almost impossible to find a member of the clergy who did not feel obliged to identify with the Council reforms. There were the minority, in the Lefèbvrist mould, who were in open conflict with ecclesiastical authority. But their stance only made things worse for the scrupulous conscience. Alfred cut clean through this Gordian knot with that simple intellectual clarity so characteristic of him. There is a wonderfully liberating distinction (admirably developed in his essay 'Fundamentals and Accidentals', appendixed to *We Believe*) which I have never heard anyone else expound, or at least develop with the same pertinence, between dogma and policy. 'The basic essentials [to quote Alfred's article] which alone command my wholehearted acceptance and loyalty' constitute the dogmatic structure of the Church; policy is everything else. We have a duty in obedience to comply with the official policies of the Church, but we are in no way obliged to give our intellectual assent to them, or *feel* loyalty in their regard. In fact, one has a duty in conscience to point out, as uncontentiously as may be, aspects of Church policy that one considers mistaken. This, discreetly and charitably, Alfred did. To listen to this wisdom was balm to many hurt consciences.

I often felt that Alfred's great practical intellectual gift was his grasp of human psychology – 'what makes people tick', to use one of his happy colloquialisms. (On a more mundane level, I remember being struck by his keen interest in the psychology of advertising.) The wisdom one was conscious of in Alfred's appreciation of Church government was the fruit of sound psychology. And it was precisely the Church's abandonment of sound psychology that struck Alfred most about the wave of reforms issuing from Vatican II. Just when the liberal misapprehensions about human nature were appearing most threadbare, the Church took them on board with seemingly naïve enthusiasm. Alfred put the matter with characteristic vigour in stating that 'for 2,000 years the Church had had human psychology taped, and she now appeared to be throwing it all out of the window overnight'. The whole normative and egalitarian thrust of Vatican II was so contrary to Church tradition. She had always known just what human nature could and couldn't take. Traditionally, she had always avoided the tendency toward arid intellectualism and narrow moralism on the one hand, and vapid sentimentalism on the other, tendencies precisely so characteristic of Protestantism. She was extraordinarily understanding of the frailties of the average sinner, and yet did not hesitate to call those capable of responding to the highest, even the most extravagant, forms of sanctity. Alfred enjoyed calling attention to contrasting examples of the call to sanctity: St Thomas More, Chancellor of England, and St Joseph of Copertino, the Italian lay-brother, with the gift of levitation (though bi-location was the only gift Alfred claimed to envy); St Joan of Arc and St Theresa of Lisieux; St Louis, King of France, and St Benedict Joseph Labre who had lived the life of a tramp.

For the whole of her history, until the inspiration of policy fell into the hands of academic theologians in the 1960s, the Church had known that human nature responds not to concepts and theories but to symbol, drama, and discipline. People expect of the higher authorities that condition their lives, eminently those of Church and State, that they should take them out of themselves onto a higher, more exciting, more dramatic plane. The grand drama of Christian Revelation needs to be fittingly dramatised. The Church's incomparable liturgical and architectural tradition did just that. She knew that in cultivating pageant, splendour and mystery she was speaking to the human heart. Christ's triumph over sin and death is the ultimate 'success story' and people long to see it celebrated; but striking a note of triumph was precisely, using the smear word 'triumphalism', what the Council reformers intended to eliminate. The insinuation was that such a note, and its accompanying modes of expression, were an offence against the spirit of poverty. But would Christians be any poorer in spirit if they did away with 'the beauty of holiness', with their sublime artistic and liturgical heritage, relegating it to museum status? Much Protestant thought has opined so, but never, until the policies of Vatican II, the Catholic Church. How the authorities of the Church could imagine that discarding the beautiful and lovingly-made vestments piously accumulated in so many sacristies, and abandoning the high altar ('altare privilegiatum') of every church, in favour of celebrating Mass 'draped in bathrobes around a kitchen table' (Alfred's pertinent caricature) would bring a pagan world flocking back to church, staggers the imagination. In fact, however, it didn't stagger

Alfred's, as he so clearly saw that an incarnate Church cannot not reflect the spirit and prejudices of the times, our *Zeitgeist* being egalitarian, as Alfred never allowed us to forget.

The discipline of the Church in regard to the faithful had been, it seemed to Alfred, just right: not too much, but demanding enough to engage respect and promote *esprit de corps* and the pride of belonging. The liberals wanted to replace the feeling of imposed discipline with the supposed authenticity of personal and spontaneous choice. Alfred pointed out the faulty psychology behind lifting the Friday abstinence rule on the expectation that the faithful would go on performing penitential acts of their own choosing. Once a practice ceases to be a rule and becomes an option, the majority of people simply end up forgetting the practice. This is at a relatively trivial level, but it has been much more disturbing to see the Church reluctant to assert her authority (presumably hoping private conscience would suffice) in such matters as respect for the Blessed Sacrament and the desirability of regular confession, as well as in the whole area of family morals and Catholic education. Alfred made one aware of the inherent contradiction in the notion of liturgical spontaneity. How does a spontaneous gesture remain spontaneous when performed for the second or third time? There was also the irony of 'the kiss of peace'. Had one ever seen this, a focus of community spontaneity in the new order of Mass, being performed other than at the celebrant's prompting?

How could a pious Catholic, attached to the continuous traditions of the Church, approve the proscription of the traditional Latin Liturgy ? Alfred's answer was that he didn't have to. The sense that the policies of the Church had been taken over by a pressure group seemed confirmed by what can only be termed an internal persecution: a purging of those recalcitrantly attached to traditional forms of liturgy and devotion. It is not uncharacteristic of supposedly liberal reformers that they talk about freeing the individual from the constraints of authority and yet do not hesitate to be ruthless in imposing their own orthodoxy. Critics of the Church like to point to what they consider inhuman policies resulting from her authoritarian nature: the suppression of the

Mark Hall, Essex. Above, from the park. Below, the smoking room.

Bishop's Hostel, Trinity College, Alfred's keeping-room, 1921

The Old Guest Room, Trinity College, 1922. Alfred at head of the table.

Alfred after blessing a memorial tablet to Sheila Kaye-Smith at St Teresa's Church, near Northiam, Sussex, 10 April 1955

Alfred chez Robert de Stacpoole, Easter 1970

Fisher House in 1965. Above, Upper Chapel. Below, The Great Chamber.

Fisher House in 1965. Above, Dining Room. Below, Library.

Alfred at the Oratory, after saying Mass on his ninetieth birthday, 13 July 1991 (photograph by Guy Lorriman)

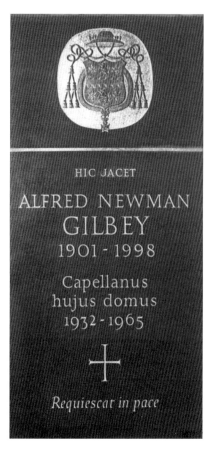

HIC JACET

ALFRED NEWMAN
GILBEY
1901 - 1998

Capellanus
hujus domus
1932 - 1965

✝

Requiescat in pace

Right, Alfred's gravestone at Fisher House

Albigensians, the brutality of the Crusades, the Inquisition, for example. But when before had we seen her persecuting her most pious and devoted members? Alfred was acutely aware that many converts (many of his own) felt betrayed, felt, as he put it, 'that the carpet had been pulled from under their feet', the Church doing away with the very characteristics that had attracted them to her.

Alfred was always there to reassure and encourage, underlining the distinction between fundamentals and accidentals, and putting matters in broader historical perspective. He pointed out that what he referred to as the 'tidy' Church of the last four centuries was exceptional, the previous centuries of her history having been constantly disturbed by divisive forces. While the Council reformers were trying to force our conscience with talk of conformity to 'the mind of the Church', Alfred encouraged us to keep our conscience free, though accepting the ascesis of obedience – that obedience which the visible Church of Christ is empowered to demand of us. One cannot overestimate the centrality in Alfred's understanding of the nature of the Church, of the notion of her being the Incarnation continued. 'Our fathers in God' exercise Apostolic authority, the Church being a 'club' whose rules you have to obey and from which, once you have grasped her *raison d'être,* you cannot resign.

Alfred was happy to point out that he continued to celebrate the Mass in the Tridentine rite because the privilege to do so had been granted him by Cardinal Heenan. He always kept the letter to that effect in his chalice box. More surprising to some will be the account he gave me of a conversation he had had at the High Table of Trinity. His neighbour had asked him what he would do if the Church allowed the ordination of women. 'If the Church said it were all right, it would be all right by me.' He clearly didn't mean that he would have wanted to promote such a policy, but he was expressing both his acceptance of ecclesiastical authority and his whole-hearted belief in the Church's guarantee of inerrancy (a term he preferred to infallibility).

Of two of the more obvious caricatural portrayals of Alfred, one is encouraged by a number of those in sympathy with him and the other by those out of sympathy with him; and one wonders whether the one encouraged by his friends isn't the more misleading. Opponents of Alfred's position tend to make him out to have been some sort of private prelate to the rich and privileged. The slur is so obvious that it is hardly disturbing. More misleading is the view, often cultivated by people friendlily disposed to him, that he was an ultramontanist attached to an authoritarian Church that Vatican II seemed to threaten, and an ardent, if somewhat dandified, exponent of 'Romanita'. This often goes with the view that his affection for the Stuart dynasty meant he was a Jacobite legitimist. This view is fundamentally to misunderstand Alfred's root inspirations, what 'made him tick'. He was a traditionalist and not a conservative. He believed that tradition was a living, growing thing that can be interrupted but cannot be turned back. One of his formulas which most influenced my own thinking was 'There is no such thing as restoration'. The immediate context of the remark was the Stuart 'restoration' of 1660. Alfred's point was that the monarchy that had gone under in 1649 was not resuscitated in 1660: the monarchical institution of 1660 was a new thing. He was deeply grateful for the hereditary monarchy we actually had. I remember him remarking that when he saw the flag flying over Buckingham Palace, knowing that the Queen was in residence, he felt deep reassurance. The Stuart dynasty may certainly have embodied a more glamorous and effective tradition but it had no exclusive claim.

Alfred deplored the administrative centralisation of the Church which had so markedly increased since the nineteenth century, and which put excessive power into the hands of the Curia. He pointed to the irony that when, as a supposed reaction to this, the idea of episcopal collegiality was being promoted, firstly it was being given a democratically consensual interpretation and, secondly, the college, being entirely composed of Curial appointees, basically 'yes men', was incapable of taking any independent stance. In the disorderly period following Vatican II, when the faithful were looking desperately to one or other of the episcopal body to give a lead, the idea of collegiality had rendered the bishops even more ineffectual. As Alfred observed: 'They spend their time looking over their shoulders at one another, fearful of seeming to be at all out of step.'

Alfred liked the distinction between the 'esse' and the 'bene esse' of the Church's organisation: the 'esse' being the secular clergy, without which the life of the Church would stop; the 'bene esse' being the regular clergy who are, as it were, the spiritual athletes of the Church and among whom the dominant tradition of the time will set the tone for the life of the Church as a whole. He contrasted the locally rooted, decentralised Benedictine tradition, dominant in the medieval period, with the deliberately rootless, Papacy-centred tradition of the Society of Jesus which had set the tone since the Counter-Reformation. Alfred's preference was certainly not for rootlessness. He preferred the family-inspired concept of the Bene-dictine community and felt that the modern custom of changing abbots and not allowing them life tenure was contrary to the patri-archal spirit of the Rule of St Benedict: 'In a family, you don't change your father.' He liked to point out that a number of English institutions, untouched by the effects of the French Revolution, remained remarkably medieval in character, in contrast to their Continental counterparts. The administrative structure of the Church of England was one example.

Alfred was an ardent defender of 'parson's freehold' which gives stability to an incumbent and avoids him becoming a bishop's pawn to be pushed about at will as the Roman clergy tend to be, precisely on the model of the relationship pertaining between a member of a religious order and his superior.

Alfred's traditionalism was more than a political or ecclesiastical preference: it was basic to his whole Catholic philosophy. A society was a living continuum which could be guided in its development but not arbitrarily manipulated by reformers. Unlike the abstract utopias of the liberal-humanists, Catholic theology was 'incarnate' in a philosophy of continuity and growth. The academic reformers of Vatican II shared with Protestantism the idea that you could go back to the supposed (academically reconstructed) forms and prac-tices of an idealised early Church and successfully substitute them for the existing state of things: what Alfred deplored as the 'archae-ological' approach. Again, the psychology was so faulty; at least Protestantism had been carried by a degree of popular support whereas the reformers of the *aggiornamento* assumed they could impose renewal purely authoritarianly, without such support. The pious feelings of large sections of the faithful, thus inevitably trampled upon, were not even presented as a necessary sacrifice: they were simply ignored.

In a similar way ecumenism seemed motivated by a nostalgic desire to revive a period in the Church's history antecedent to the Protestant revolution and the consequent more explicit assertion of the exclusive claims of the See of Peter. Alfred objected that the current ecumenism tended to be both uncharitable and demoralising. To play down the differences between the Church and other Christian bodies, particularly the fundamental one of her being the original and indivisible Mystical Body, and to go on to give the impression that everyone was on an equal footing on the path to recovering a lost unity was in danger of being culpably misleading. When circumstances arose, as they inevitably would do, pressing the Church to come out in her true, exclusive colours, the non-Catholic partners of the ecumenical dialogue would inevitably feel a sense of betrayal, of having been 'led up the garden path'. Again, Alfred was conscious of the debilitating effects of ecumenism. Glossing over differences and diluting identity is not conducive to good morale. In this regard he reminded us of the Pauline admonition: 'If the trumpet shall give forth an uncertain sound, who shall go to battle?'

Alfred was very conscious that previous renewals in the Church's history had sprung from a renewal of spirituality; here we had the attempt to base renewal on intellectual constructs and the manipulation of liturgical forms, with the impression given that these changes were at a fundamental level of the life in the Church: 'fashion masquerading as principle' was Alfred's luminous phrase. What comfort was Alfred able to bring to the many who were hurt and bewildered by these brutal upheavals? It was a comfort to be reminded of the broader historical context and also of the Divine character of the Church; it was a special comfort to witness his own heroic serenity. The 'archaeologising' of Vatican II was simply a logical step in the historicist obsession that had gripped the mind of the West since the nineteenth century. The whole Gothic Revival had been an expression of it – though, as Alfred indicated, without the devastating aesthetic effects of the current innovations. He also suggested that the pain occasioned to so many by the present changes could hardly compare with the distress that must have been felt at the time of the dissolution of the monasteries, which wiped out not only liturgical forms but a whole way of life. Unlike all other societies, the Church, as the Body of Christ, enjoys a principle of unity and continuity which is a greater reality than the individuals and constituent authorities composing her, or the agreements or disagreements between them. This is as much as to say that whereas other human societies cannot survive revolutionary change, the Church can. Alfred's aesthetic sense was intensely visual (he admitted no enjoyment of music, being 'tone deaf') and to see the beautiful and venerable forms of the Church he loved suffering a sort of self-mutilation was deeply offensive to him; but it never affected his serenity and joyful confidence.

One could venture to sum up Alfred's psychological insight into the life of the Church as the knowledge that religion appeals to those levels of personality engaged rather by poetry than prose. Whereas Protestantism had been a deliberate attempt to rationalise Christianity, the traditional ritual of the Church had always favoured the poetry of pageant and mystery. A rationalist reformer might reply that the practicalities of Christian charity tend to be prosaic. One could respond that Christian charity, as opposed to humanist philanthropy, is characterised by a commitment of the heart inspired by the 'poetry' of living faith. A prosaic liturgy is a contradiction in terms.

To understand better Alfred's temperament and field of action, there is an illuminating remark about himself which merits the sort of distinction of meaning that he would have liked. He said of his four brothers (all laymen) that two had had religion worse than he and two less badly. He was using the term 'religion' with its familiar reference to theology, pious practices (the two religious brothers travelled the country persuading Catholic households to 'enthrone the Sacred Heart') and things ecclesiastical. Alfred was not exclusively interested in religious matters in this sense. He was religious in the more original sense of the word: his wider interests in civilisation as man perfecting nature, and in the rhythms and harmonies of the natural world, were inspired by that religious reverence or awe (a word he loved) that derives from the sense of the all-permeating presence of God. I remember on one occasion beagling with him near Cambridge and his admiring the blue sky sweeping down vertically onto the flat expanse of the fens: 'Las obras del Senor!' he exclaimed, quoting his mother. The healing impact of Alfred's message and personality was situated precisely at the meeting point between nature and supernature. This is what made Alfred such a reconciler and bridger of gaps. He was one of the rare people, and rare clerics, able to make one feel at ease with God and man.

'The two books that I *never* wrote' (*We Believe* and *The Commonplace Book*) reflect the two dimensions of his interests: supernatural and natural, theological and, in a non-academic sense, philosophical. This balance and the feeling that Alfred's thought echoed, all the more because of its rootedness, a universal wisdom helped some of us enjoy the fascination of traditions outside Christianity, without any feeling of being in conflict with one's Catholic Faith. This was paradoxical, as Alfred always declared himself unattracted to civilisations other than Christian – an exception being the first architectural love of his childhood, the Taj Mahal. The focus of Alfred's intellectual approach was the necessity of getting back to first principles, his capacity for which brought light to many in the contemporary liberal-humanist fog. Again, one felt that the breadth and vigour of his thought in this regard sprang from something deeper than simply the rational inclination of the Latin mind. His thought was in line with all traditional wisdom in its claim that there are foundation certainties, with inescapable consequences, necessitating clear choices. What a contrast to the liberal-humanist stance! To quote one of Alfred's illuminating definitions: 'The liberal-humanist starts from no declared premise, determined to reach no certain conclusions.'

One thing liberal-humanist thought loses is the notion of clear identity and relationships, hence its inevitable egalitarian slide. Alfred's clarity had once more a liberating effect. He helped restore credibility to the traditional relationships between God and man, man and woman, man and the 'lower creation'. He was awed at the sublimity of the truth that value is given to existence through the co-operation of two wills: man's and his Creator's. Hence Alfred's deep attachment to the foundation institution, and indispensable framework for that co-operation: the family. 'Without the family there is no love, and without property there is no freedom.' One of Alfred's perfect statements and, one would have thought, a self-evident truth; but a truth that the Godless, 'omnicompetent' state is determined to forge. Alfred reaffirmed the truths that are so obvious that a whole civilisation can forget them. In the contentious area of the feminine role in society, it is an absurd distortion to present the traditional view as belittling women. Again, the liberals won't accept basic psychology. The complementary roles of the sexes assume their difference and a healthy society requires customs and institutions that affirm that difference: all wearing the same clothes, being identically educated, and belonging to the same clubs and colleges, is conducive neither to nurturing the different emotional needs of the sexes, nor to promoting a genuine complementarity between them. The notion, so mocked at, that woman's place is in the home is simply the corollary of her being most fulfilled by motherhood. The post-Christian West actively invites women to that sterility which all traditional societies have considered a curse. As my son, an ardent admirer of Alfred – as not a few in their twenties are – remarked: 'Home is where the mother is.'

If there was one enthusiasm of Alfred's most emblematic of the traditionalist balance of his views, it was certainly hunting, which, since his undergraduate days at Cambridge, took the form of beagling. I remember Alfred commenting on the isolated enclave of Catholicism that his home, Mark Hall, represented in the Essex countryside: 'a world which was entirely a-Catholic and whose religion was fox-hunting'. His father was a dedicated member of the Essex Hunt and Alfred had hunting in his blood from his father – as he claimed sherry ran in his veins from his mother. The English country gentleman with his rural pursuits was a high expression of that view of civilisation that sees a balanced relationship between man and his natural environment as fundamental. The colour and drama of the chase has always been seen as a way in which man enters into a dynamic relationship with the realities of the natural world, and, in a symbolic way, with his own nature. Again, without a religious foundation the arguments in favour of field sports involving the death of the quarry fall short of conviction (the 'culling' argument, for instance). As Alfred pointed out, man needs to be in a right relationship as well with the realities below him as with those above him. 'Man has sovereignty over the lower creation' he reminded one. The death of the quarry is the climax of the chase and its symbolic focus: a fulfilment of the natural cycle of life and death and reminding man that he too, at his level, is caught up in that cycle.

One of the most romantic events in Alfred's calendar was his annual trip to Northumberland in September with the TFB (Trinity Foot Beagles). On a number of occasions I had the privilege of accompanying him on this outing. There is a wonderful remote beauty about the Northumbrian countryside with the line of the bare hills so sharply etched against the clear purity of the sky. We stayed in a charming country pub in Thropton, where, by good fortune, within two minutes' walk was a fine stone chapel in the Gothic style, set back from the road with recusant discretion. We would read the hunting passages from 'Sir Gawayne and the Greene Knight' in which Sir Gawayne always heard Mass before setting out for the chase. We did likewise, rising at what seemed the crack of dawn, so that there was time for dressing (the tying and pinning of Alfred's stock was not something to be hurried), the celebration of Mass and breakfast before joining an early meet at eight o'clock. Beagling, because more intimate in style (on foot and over a limited circle of ground) than fox-hunting, seems especially eloquent in expressing the desirable harmonies between man and nature. Alfred's elegant figure, leaning on his stick on a Northumbrian hillside observing the chase, in his black waisted jacket, spotted blue Essex Hunt waistcoat, fawn riding breeches, spats, tweed cap and immaculate white stock seemed a focus of such harmonies.

Alfred was not without his failings: a certain stubbornness, even complacency, and a life-long ineffectiveness where administrative tasks, particularly correspondence, were concerned. His attachment to ritual had its picturesque but, to some degree, inhibiting excesses: the elaborate precision-work of the frequent packing and unpacking, the above average hand-washing, and the accompanying Pear's soap ritual – but, above all, his 'second levée'. Having said Mass and breakfasted, a sizeable portion of his mid-morning was taken up with the change from cassock to clerical suit and accompanying ablutions. By the time this was finished, he was working up to his first appointment of the day, followed invariably by a luncheon engagement. He had lost just that section of the day so conveniently suited to 'admin'. It could seem discouraging to some who were struggling to generate prosperity for their families when Alfred denounced (right though he undoubtedly was) avarice (not sexual disorder) as the controlling vice of the age, particularly coming from a man enjoying a substantial private fortune. It could seem almost provocatively convenient for a man clearly more emotionally comfortable with members of his own sex so confidently to champion all-male institutions. For one of so positive an outlook and so happily established, Alfred's insistence that our feelings were of no importance in comparison to the disposition of the will could seem to some, less fortunately placed, rather disconcerting. He was in fact a man of notable generosity, of profound personal integrity, and of tender solicitude towards friends in distress. Nevertheless, a note of apparent complacency could sometimes exasperate. There is a sense in which those who loved Alfred would not have wanted him without his faults, not because one approved of them, but because his realism and humility about them made his humanity all the more vivid and touching. One could say that holiness rather overcomes than eliminates faults: it removes their viciousness, while leaving some of their troublesome effects to discourage pride. Alfred liked to quote Abbot Herbert Byrne of Ampleforth (Abbot 1939–63). He had remarked to him: 'I sometimes feel so inadequate, Father Abbot.' 'It would be a sorry day if one ever felt adequate' responded Abbot Byrne.

Alfred's extraordinary balance of cultural and temperamental qualities gave him his inimitable poise, charm and serenity. In this balance he managed to harmonise and make accessible 'the beauty of holiness' and the attractions of civilisation. He helped those about him 'love the highest when they saw it'. His specific apostolate was precisely to those most in need of an embodiment of high values, the aspiring middle classes, who were the great majority of his flock at Fisher House and in London, a fact in contradiction of the parody of his being some sort of chaplain to upper-class Catholics. The fact that he was acceptable to the higher spheres of English society can only be viewed as a remarkable asset for the Catholic Church in England, though inadequately appreciated.

Alfred's sustained vitality and self-giving is inconceivable without a certain asceticism. Physically, there was a tireless accessibility to others: at Cambridge, open house to his flock from morning beyond midnight; at the Travellers' the endless stream of visitors, the never-ending phone-calls, the ceaseless entertaining. Then there was his entire commitment to the sacramental ministry, reaching the heroic proportions of rising, still in his ninety-seventh year, at 5.30 a.m. in order to celebrate Mass for his devoted congregation at 7.30 a.m. at the Oratory. Morally, in illustration of his maxim 'worry is a sin', one could observe his unshakeable and, one can only say, joyful serenity, despite living a century of the cataclysmic collapse of all the civilised forms he loved.

The force and magic of Alfred's personality derived from his ability to hold in a sort of 'poetic tension' a number of rich dualities: Spain and England, Catholicism and Anglicanism, the supernatural and natural planes. But the full reach of his personality stretched to the ultimate test of harmony: the point of balance between time and eternity – the point where sanctity is found. If Alfred had a negative obsession – egalitarianism – he also had a positive one, the present moment. Alfred's wisdom could perhaps be summarised in his insistence on the necessity of living in and sanctifying the present moment. One of his favourite passages was from C. S. Lewis's *The Screwtape Letters*, where the apprentice devil is told by his master at all costs to keep human beings' attention (preferably plunged in regret and worry) away from the present moment, that moment which alone is real and in which time and eternity intersect. He also had a particular appreciation of the concluding words of the Hail Mary – 'pray for us now and at the hour of our death': our two most vital moments.

Alfred made an illuminating distinction between goodness and holiness. He had observed it in the life of his dearly loved nurse, Antonia. She had remained a spinster and had put all her energies into devoted service to the Gilbey family. Her life had been eminently good and un-self-centred. In her old age she had lived with Alfred at Fisher House and it was there that she suffered a severe stroke. She spent the last six months of her life in the Evelyn Nursing Home, lying paralysed and unable to speak. Alfred said that during that time he saw something beyond goodness: he saw her visibly growing in holiness in her complete abandonment to God.

Alfred died at the age of ninety-seven, having enjoyed remarkably good health into his nineties, decrepitude only setting in in the last three or four years. He accepted it patiently and without complaint, battling to maintain his pattern of life (he was beagling in Northumberland in September 1997) and showing remarkable resilience after several crashing, though miraculously not bone-breaking, falls. The move from the Travellers' Club to a convent nursing-home at the end of January 1998 was not of his choosing but he accepted it with generous resignation. He died at the end of March. But something happened in those last two months which I, for circumstances beyond my control, was only able to witness at a distance (at the end of a telephone line in fact) but which others saw. There seemed a flowering of holiness. For me, his simple counsels had a fresh immediacy. He was so pleased to have got his own telephone line. The last thing he said to me was: 'I wish people [in distress] knew they had a "hot-line" here. I want to tell them that all you need to do is put God in the centre and the rest will come right.' Alfred died present to the present moment and centred in God.

Gilbert Monckton

In my last term at Harrow I thought of the Catholic Church. In the holidays afterwards in Sicily two priests walked slowly down the beach, dressed in thick black clothes; everyone else was naked or in summer shorts. My mother and sister met them and I later. They came from St Mary's, Chorley; one was Dr Flynn, later Bishop of Lancaster. I stayed with them, wonderful food and drink. On asking how I could join the Roman Catholic Church, I was told to call on Father Gilbey in my first term at Trinity. Thus I met my mentor and friend for life. To be honest I thought I would sign a paper and then become a Catholic!

The first meeting was social and discovering mutual friends and interests, the next day was a serious examination – personal past and hopes for the future. Then the instruction began over many days and was 'thorough'. Confession lasted for most of one morning and the relief of losing so many sins of the past removed a heavy burden. Throughout, both at Fisher House and the local restaurants, his hospitality was inspiring. At last the day came when I was received into the Church with the full approval of my parents.

Trinity College meant a lot to us, as did the Trinity Foot Beagles. Alfred always knew where the hunt could be watched and which way the hunt would go. The hunt staff were all his friends. Thus clubs and societies always wanted him and some he founded himself. He was a member of the Pitt Club and many others. He started the Strafford Club to honour Thomas Wentworth and the Whip Club to encourage driving. We drove to Newmarket for the races and to local hunt races.

At one stage for one term I hunted six days a week but ended with a crashing fall and cracked skull. I woke up some days later to find Alfred giving me the Last Rites and my mother on the other side. Alfred had time for all and was tireless in helping those in difficulties.

In the war after Dunkirk I tried to join the RAF as there was no role for the Army. I failed the eye test but was made an Air Liaison officer and sent on a course to Cambridge. Once more Alfred gave all by letting me stay with him at Fisher House and I fear giving me some of his rations. There were some wild parties but the anchor was, as always, Alfred. We kept in touch wherever I was posted.

At the end of 1950 I got married by the Bishop of Lancaster. Alfred said the Mass and we had breakfast together before the ceremony. He came to our anniversaries wherever we were, except Korea and Egypt. We could not meet very often and one of the last times was at a Trinity Reunion for the old and I was not very fit. Alfred noticed and organised a suitable medicine before dinner, a bottle of champagne for each of us.

I apologise for so personal an account, Alfred helped so many others in similar ways. He was not only a party man, above all he was a holy man devoted to the Church and to God. It would be interesting to know how many young men he received into the Church. I thank all those who helped him in his declining years. I thank God for Alfred's life. May he rest in peace.

John Patten

[Lord Patten was a member of Monsignor Gilbey's flock at Fisher House whilst he was an undergraduate and then a postgraduate at Sidney Sussex between 1964 and 1969.]

A. N. GILBEY AND PROPER CONDUCT

Who was the last person invariably to raise his hat when passing the Cenotaph in Whitehall, whether on foot, in a car, or in a bus? Yet who was also the last person whilst wearing that highly recognisable hat, to hawk, albeit with grace, into the gutter as he walked rapidly along Pall Mall? To the best of my knowledge in both cases, it was Monsignor Gilbey. As such, these activities were part of his intricate system of proper conduct; for each of which there was an explanation if only you asked. They were not only permissible; they were perfected and correct by virtue of being perfected.

Proper conduct provided a framework for his life, and the driving force behind his attitude towards others, just as his clear sense of the importance of hierarchy allowed him to order the world around him in its turn. Monsignor Gilbey was grand, but he did not fulfil the *Oxford English Dictionary* definition of a snob ('One whose ideas and conduct are prompted by the vulgar admiration for wealth or social position').

He knew of the frequent combination of the socialist and the snob, for example, and disliked it very much. His overwhelming belief in hierarchy meant that he could place everyone in his mind's eye in their proper place. Yet to everyone his conduct seemed invariably to be impeccable, over the thirty-five years that I knew him. For he treated all with natural, graceful and unforced courtesy; that was his starting point. In the Gilbean code, therefore, to believe in hierarchies and the natural order of things did not mean snobbery, did not allow for the patronising nor the aloof. In this respect, he was unusual amongst that gallery of twentieth-century English priests whose adopted parish was the London *ton* of the day. If there were some to whom might be attributed the cruel confessional joke of 'Bless me, Father, for I have sinned, it is six months since my last Confession, and I have committed adultery with a lady.' 'A lady, Lady *whom* …?', it was not Gilbey.

There was no obviously tiresome *noblesse oblige* as part of his code of conduct towards other people. For to lean over backwards to be kind would mean becoming patronising in the process. Rather he treated every waiter in the Travellers' Club, or elsewhere, with exactly the same consideration that he treated visiting grandees. But then, he treated prisoners in exactly the same careful way when he was a young priest in the Brentwood Diocese, and was sent by his Bishop to visit the local jail regularly. And with whomsoever, the rule was always to look them in the eye, at least until increasing age made this task the more and more challenging as he, in his turn, bent more and more towards the table.

Most of his rules or code of conduct were directed towards men, for it was in male company that he rejoiced as an old-fashioned bachelor, as well as priest. It is to his men friends that he looked for help in order to 'keep the jungle at bay'; or whom he lectured on the necessity of achieving this task. Women, to Monsignor Gilbey, were another species – but a species to be treated with particular courtesy, once their place or role in life had been established. He adored, sometimes worshipped it seemed from conversation, his mother. From her he had inherited those overhanging and hooded eyelids which made his face, even when it began to line and drop, so very striking and handsome. (He clipped his eyelashes until near the end.)

To some his attitude towards the female species might seem contradictory. His courtesy, not to say sometimes elaborate politeness towards and consideration for women, raised them to a pinnacle, but also at the same time placed them into an essentially parallel position in the hierarchy to men. His attitude to, and devotion to the memory of, his own mother led him to position women, when appropriate, on a pedestal of motherhood.; to thus stress the importance of one's own mother in particular; and of Catholic families in general. In this he regarded Cardinal Manning as having had the first, and the last, word on the subject in his *Towards Evening*: 'To put man and woman upon an equality is not to elevate woman but to degrade her. I trust that the womanhood of England, to say nothing of the Christian conscience which yet remains, will resist by a stern moral refusal the immodesty which would thrust women from their private life of duty and supremacy into the public conflicts of men.'

Yet in the company of women, across the dinner table, he was usually not just courtesy, but often gaiety itself. Whenever we met, one of the first questions which he would ask was 'How is your dear Louise ... and your daughter?' He rarely spent much time alone with women, though 'my dear Louise' has never forgotten those hours that she did spend with him as a result of her having won a scholarship to St Paul's Girls School in London. There, in a muddled way, her Confirmation as a cradle Catholic had simply been forgotten. As a result, and quite properly, he took the view that no proper Catholic marriage could take place (as it later did in the Lady Chapel of Westminster Cathedral on American Independence Day 1978, Monsignor Gilbey celebrating and Dom James Forbes, O.S.B. preaching) until the, to him curious, oversight had been put right.

This led to her summons by him for a series of instructions, in preparation for the belated ceremony, seated in the morning room of the Travellers' Club, the previous spring and early summer. The great sash windows were open onto the street, and thus in their turn open to the noise of the taxis and No 11 buses in full flood outside. Monsignor Gilbey was bent over the beloved 'Penny Catechism' of his youth, which he occasionally took up to underline with vigour – but in pencil – while she in her turn strained each time to hear the rapid and quick-fire instruction, delivered in what some (not unkindly) later characterised as approximating to Serbo-Croat murmured through a damp blanket. But all was delivered with a purpose; to bring about Confirmation; to help with the cure of this particular female soul; and to inculcate with exquisite politeness that she should at least recall the proper role of women, without for one second falling into the vulgarity of telling her what to do. And all from a face which already was taking on that characteristic look which was remarkably close to the ancient Cardinal Manning's, as described by G. K. Chesterton: '... his face was dead pale like ivory and very wrinkled and old, fitted together out of naked nerve and bone and sinew; with hollow eyes in shadow; but not ugly; having in every line the ruin of great beauty.'

It was to men that he was much more inclined to be the more didactic. Much instruction happened from the pulpit, very hard though it sometimes was to catch every word. But much also happened around the luncheon table, or over dinner. Underlying almost everything he said about conduct was his lack of snobbery, and his contempt for it. This seemed to be grounded in his innate Toryism – and I seek not to explain him thus for any party political reason. One of his favourite passages was Osbert Burdett on the issue: 'The true Tory cannot be a snob. The Tory recognises that all good things are abuses, that the finer the thing the worse is the abuse; but he never confuses the abuse with the thing itself, nor attacks the one without distinguishing it from the other.' Thus to be interested in heraldry was to be concerned with the intricacies and elaborations of order, genealogy and a sense of place, spiced with a lot of style. It was most definitely concerned with hierarchy and family; equally definitely, it was not about snobbery. The systems underpinning heraldry rather are about correct conduct. And correct interpretation; thus when I asked Monsignor Gilbey of the significance of a heraldic device carved into an elaborate (and delightfully adjustable) Gothic chair that we had just purchased, back came the answer, 'Why it has a punning shell ...' And, a little later, came why, with Gilbey's complete account:

Hervey Charles Pechell of Maresfield Park, Sussex
b. 19. August 1841 3rd. son of Horace Robert Pechell, who

was 2nd. son of Sir Paul Pechell, 1st. Bt. (cr. 1. March 1797)
married 12. November 1874
Blanche Henrietta Johnes only child and heir of Sir John Vil-
liers
 Shelleg, 7th. Bt.
 There were no children of the marriage.
 He died 28. December 1898.
 She died 12. April 1898.

A proper attitude to dining properly and well – but not indul-
gently – was also of critical importance to Monsignor Gilbey. The
very way of choosing a dinner underlay proper conduct. In this he
seemed to give faint echo to his Lordship at home in Holland
House, who, having given a young man the opportunity to pick his
dinner, and who in his turn chose duck and green peas with an apri-
cot tart, was treated with the rejoinder: '... If in all the important
questions of your life you decide as wisely as you have decided now,
you will be a great and good man.' Thus followed from Monsignor
Gilbey a clear instruction to the young unused to the proper way of
choosing dinner – but with infinite caution and suggestibility – the
idea that it really was not *quite right* to look to how one might
start. It was wrong to let everything flow from that soup or those
potted shrimps. Rather, the instruction ran – and almost with the
intensity of more important matters being inculcated into some
postulant for the Church – that one really should start in the
middle, and build the rest around the meat. And that was generally
very well grilled lamb cutlets, or occasionally if some trolley or
another was flourished, those bits of beef the colour of an old
mahogany table exactly as he had learnt to enjoy at his parents'
table in Essex. The conduct of eating for him was thus the orderly
choice of good food, but plain, preferably accompanied by one
wine, and best of all not a muddle of different sorts of glasses. By all
means sherry before, and sometimes (though less and less with the
passing of the years) port afterwards, as befits someone from his
wine merchant's lineage, but always claret with food; and sometimes quite a great deal of that too. Yet I never remember high

spirits and gay conversation crossing that social frontier zone into anything remotely approximating to drunkenness. Neither do I recall, nor have I ever met, anyone who has attributed that to Monsignor Gilbey. This was the restraint born of a code that was born not of tiresome nor bourgeois 'good manners', but rather how you should enjoy yourself with a sense of dignity and a care for others, according to the clearest code of conduct.

Neither was tiresome standing back nor equally tiresome ushering forward to be encouraged. Hosts should walk boldly into club coffee room or restaurant, in order to deal with choice of table and table plan alike. It was the same in the matter of getting out of lifts, always first before your guests to show them the way, or, if one was a lady, to help her from this particular form of conveyance as though down from coach or railway carriage door.

Physical contact was neither encouraged nor discouraged, but should happen according to what was simply right. An embrace, or a kiss on the cheek, to an old friend, was unaffected warmth on stilts, nothing more, nothing less. And when sharing an umbrella in the street, the automatic linking of arms in order to make sheltering from the rain that bit easier was natural and proper whether or not you knew someone well. There should be no embarrassment in this. It was just good conduct.

Everything had its proper place in Monsignor Gilbey's code. Nothing was forgotten, even the humble postage stamp (invariably those with the Monarch's head alone; never one of the new breed of garish commemorative stamps forced on a sometimes unwilling public by Postmaster General Wedgwood Benn). Thus, whilst he was still in the habit of sending Christmas cards to those of his more farther-flung flock with whom he wished to keep in touch, people would be dragooned into the business of affixing the stamps. A demonstration was given. Always just so. This was quite properly towards the top of the right hand corner of the envelope as is conventional, but always straight, done with care and precision – in this case 'just so' meant set well, too, into the body of the envelope itself so that it assumed its own curious kind of unforced elegance. Why? To do this simply demonstrated good manners by

showing care – and thus all the more it was a pleasure to open the
envelope once the characteristic, if increasingly shaky, black-inked
handwriting had been recognised. And how much more so it must
have been for that old friend in Cheval Place in London to get such
an envelope complete with the traditional (if highly unlikely) child-
like drawing of a horse's head next to the first line of the address,
with which Monsignor Gilbey decorated the finished article.

In all of this, and underpinned by the characteristic Gilbean code
of conduct, therefore, was a clear recognition that everything had
its place, in the hierarchy, but that everything should be treated
with respect. That understanding of people, things, and their place
ran through his life like a silver thread. Everybody, just like everything, should be accorded its proper respect. Thus the importance
of talking to a shivering and unhappy young prisoner in a squalid
Essex jail with courtesy and directness, as much as helping an
undergraduate uncertain exactly how to behave. It was Monsignor
Gilbey, when passing through Reading railway station, who always
said a prayer for 'poor Oscar Wilde' as soon as the turrets and red
brick walls of the prison came into view from the carriage window.
Thus instinctively remembering the horrors of those terrified but
brave young falling into the mud of Flanders and the Somme every
time you pass the Cenotaph. Thus remembering the old jokes and
those who liked to make them – as in when something faintly slang-
like fell from anyone's lips often remarking 'as Dr X always says
…', Dr X being a person who never, ever used slang. But thus,
through such conduct born of habit and thought also remembering
your Maker, and your place in his design.

David Watkin

Having had the honour of Alfred's friendship for thirty-six years, my contribution to this book is an account of some of his secular activities and interests during that time. I have, of course, also drawn on his numerous accounts to me of earlier periods of his life. On several of his many interests, including heraldry and beagling, I am scarcely competent to enlarge. However, it is interesting to note that before his ambition to become a priest, conceived at the age of fourteen, his greatest hope was to become a Herald. In promotion of this ambition, his father took him, at his request, on a visit to the College of Arms in Queen Victoria Street, London. In response to another request from Alfred, his father wrote at about this time to Lord Salisbury, asking if he might allow Alfred to indulge his youthful enthusiasm for Elizabethan architecture by visiting Hatfield House, not very far from Mark Hall. With the lordly grandeur of the higher peerage in the last few years before 1914, permission was declined.

Nor do I describe what was central to Alfred: his life as a priest and as a man of prayer. This has been admirably evoked in the present book by Ronald Creighton-Jobe. Anyone who reads my contribution should bear that aspect of Alfred's life constantly in mind, or he will be in danger of forming a trivial picture of a great and holy priest. Nonetheless, Alfred believed that we have a duty to enjoy the things of this world because they have been created by God, but that, being of this world, they are temporal toys.

I met Alfred for the first time on Tuesday 15 May 1962 when he came to dine in Wychfield, a large late-Victorian Arts and Crafts house built for the Darwins in Huntingdon Road where, with a group of undergraduate friends including Alastair Langlands,

Francis Annett and Ian Bonner, I was spending a blissful year reading History of Art at Trinity Hall. We had the service of a college gyp and his wife, and a garden of several acres with our own croquet lawn. Trinity Hall has since ruined the place utterly by building hideous modern buildings in the gardens by the Arup partnership, but then it was a secret idyll where we gave our own May Ball, held play readings by candlelight on the verandah on Sunday nights, and gave occasional dinner parties in my room, the drawing room of the old house.

Alfred was invited at the suggestion of Ian Bonner who had recently been converted to the Catholic Church while a boy at the Perse School. The food was not, in retrospect, anything that can have greatly appealed to Alfred. Do I remember cold ham and salami, mayonnaise, probably bottled and tasting of vinegar, possibly Alfred's greatest hate in life; and was there something from a tin labelled 'Mexican rice'? Doubtless there would have been less bread than Alfred would have wished, while the wine would have been nothing special, but that, oddly, would have worried Alfred least of all. While possessing an educated palate and capable of recognising fine wine, he was always entirely happy with modest wine. This was not, I think, the result of any desire for mortification, as were many of his private practices, but for integration into a traditional Catholic Mediterranean culture based on ordinary, local, bread and wine.

Alfred subsequently told me that he was frightened of meeting me, for he was constantly being shown off by Catholic undergraduates to their non-Catholic friends who were thought to be clever. But, though I was not only non-Catholic but non-Christian, I, like everyone who met him, was instantly captivated by his devastating charm, his warmth, his humour, his intelligence and wide reading, lightly borne. In a word, he had what is known as a charismatic personality; I had never met anyone remotely like him in my life. My attraction was partly based on the fact that, after his religion, his greatest passion in life was, like mine, architecture, particularly seen as part of social history. At this first meeting, I scribbled down notes of his conversation on the back of the programme for a

Footlights Smoking Concert of the previous evening at which Alastair Langlands and I, as well as Tim Brooke-Taylor, John Cleese, Humphry Barclay and Richard Stillgoe, had all performed. I have the programme still. The notes which I made on it of what Alfred told me include the errors in Pevsner's description of St Edmund's House in the Cambridgeshire volume of the *Buildings of England* series. Here, Alfred told me, 'Pevsner had made three mistakes in as many lines: the wrong date, the wrong architect, and the erroneous claim that it had begun life as a private house.' This last error would have been inconceivable for anyone who had seen this grimly institutional building, which Pevsner manifestly had not. No less inaccurate was Pevsner's statement that the architect was Lutyens whereas, as Alfred told me, it was Father Benedict Williamson, also architect of St Ignatius, Stamford Hill, and of the chapel at Hare Street House, Essex, built to commemorate Hugh Benson. I was already an enthusiastic admirer of Benson's novels of Edwardian life, though I did not yet know that he had been Alfred's role model on his ordination under his own patrimony as a priest.

Further information from Alfred which I also scribbled down on the same Footlights programme was that there was 'a little-known house near Cambridge, Childerley Hall, of c.1600, which had been reduced in size in 1850'. Our love of architecture and of Cambridge formed the basis of our long and intimate friendship. Moreover, the notes I made that night were an extraordinary harbinger of my future career: I was to become a Catholic within a year; to live at St Edmund's House, so ineptly described by Professor Pevsner; to become a research student of Pevsner and in due course to write a book critical of his approach; and to make annual visits to Childerley Hall for the summer picnic of the Strafford Club which Alfred had founded in 1939 and of which he appointed me Secretary.

Alfred always said that though he was known for his remarkable number of converts, he had never directly converted anyone, still less proselytised, but had simply instructed anyone who asked him to. This was true in my case. Even before I met him I had been much influenced by a book I had just bought while at Trinity Hall called *The Age of Grandeur: Baroque and Classicism in Europe*.

Written by a French scholar, Victor Tapié, it had been published in
1960 in a translation from the French. I was captivated by the
notion that the magnificent architectural and decorative Baroque
style, the one by which I was most excited, was embodied in the
forms and ritual of an institution which survived to the present day
as a continuation of the Roman Empire in the form of an absolute
monarchy, the papacy. Always attracted by splendour and hierarchy, I disapproved of socialism, egalitarianism, and Protestantism
which I saw as dominated by the singing of sentimentally worded
Victorian hymns which I had sung daily at school. The Catholic
Church, then, its pomp as 'one with Nineveh and Tyre', was what I
wanted to be part of.

Our group from Trinity Hall travelled in Italy in the summer of
1962, including a triumphal visit to Rome. On our return two of us,
my dear friend Francis Annett and I, asked Alfred, whom we all
knew at this time as 'Father Gilbey', to instruct us in the Faith. This
he did in the Michaelmas Term 1962 and Lent Term 1963. My only
fear was that he would seek to begin or end our meetings with sentimental, extempore, vernacular prayer. Happily, there was nothing
of that kind whatever in his series of workmanlike expositions. We
were received into the Catholic Church in the Upper Chapel at
Fisher House on Wednesday 22 May 1963, being given conditional
baptism with water from the silver ewer from Alfred's former home,
Mark Hall, which he always used for this purpose. How could we
know that the face of the Church to which we were admitted was
about to be utterly changed in a process which involved the destruction of everything that had attracted me to it in the first place?

From the Michaelmas Term 1963 when I became a research student at Trinity Hall, I spent the greater part of every day at Fisher
House until Alfred's enforced departure in December 1965. At a
desk in the library, below a mezzotint of Lawrence's portrait of
George IV, which had hung in the smoking room at Mark Hall, I
wrote much of my Ph. D thesis on Thomas Hope, constantly watching Alfred's comings and goings. I remember his asking me early on
why I was working on Hope because, he said, 'he was not a man of
ideas'. Alfred would have been immensely distressed had he known

how much this upset me because he spent his life trying not to cause offence to people. However, I was in the end grateful to him for I became determined to show that Hope was a serious intellectual, a 'man of ideas'. Indeed, I even called my thesis, when it was published by John Murray in 1968, *Thomas Hope (1769–1831) and the Neo-Classical Idea*.

When Alfred resigned from the chaplaincy, a victim of Vatican II, though he would not have put it like this, he was a vigorous man of sixty-four, still at the height of all his powers, physical, spiritual, emotional, and intellectual. He had devoted his life and his fortune to maintaining and improving Fisher House, and I think he had never supposed he would leave it. At that time he seemed seriously to think that his wish would be granted of dying on his seventieth birthday while carrying his suitcases up the steps at the entrance of the Athenaeum. When speaking of this strange ambition, he used to groan and swing his arms in imitation of the strain of raising the cases. So far as I could see, he had no made no preparations whatever for life after Cambridge, a place to which he had been passionately devoted from the age of eighteen. But he had iron self-control and, unlike me, lost no sleep during the period of opposition to his chaplaincy, orchestrated from St Edmund's House by a research student called John Oliver. His life of prayer and his absolute trust in divine providence enabled him to leave Cambridge in December 1965, seemingly with no regret and certainly with no bitterness.

Alastair Langlands drove Alfred and me from Cambridge that day in his beautiful 1937 Rolls-Royce to stay with his parents in their house at Stanmore. Here we spent the first night of what was to be Alfred's long 'retirement' of thirty-three years, just the time he had spent as chaplain. From Stanmore he took up residence in the Athenaeum, considering a number of opportunities of employment, the most serious being chaplain in the Guards Barracks in Birdcage Walk. Other places to which he considered moving included Pinehurst, in Grange Road, Cambridge, a gloomy block of flats where his friend, Sir Penrose Fry, Bt., resided. A modest and gentle figure, born in 1892, Fry had married the popular novelist Sheila Kaye-Smith, now best known for being parodied in *Cold Comfort Farm* by Stella Gibbons. Fry acted ineffectively as Alfred's secretary in the Oak Room at Fisher House, 'driving a typewriter', as Alfred put it. Alfred and I had tea with him at Pinehurst, I concealing a tape measure with which, at Alfred's request, I measured the drawing room, when Penrose had temporarily withdrawn, to see if it would take Alfred's favourite piece of furniture, his Regency wine table.

By accident rather than design, Alfred remained at the Athenaeum where he was amused by the pedantic donnish rules by which members could not occupy a club bedroom for more than ten nights consecutively. On alternate Mondays to Fridays, he packed his bags and indulged in what he called 'sleeping rough', that is at Cambridge, at an hotel, or with friends. However, after a while he joined the Travellers' where in 1970 a new friend, the Secretary, Robin McDouall, enabled him to have a room on a permanent basis and, eventually, even a chapel in the attic storey.

It was from this base that I saw Alfred constantly throughout the 1960s and 70s, the period when I was privileged to spend most time with him, for, as a research student and subsequently Research Fellow at Peterhouse, as yet unencumbered by membership of committees, I had much free time. Alfred would meet me at Liverpool Street Station, a favourite building of his about which he enjoyed weaving the fantasy that it was an English monastic cathedral with its Early English nave, crossed by a raised walkway serving as the slype – the high gallery by which monks passed from their dormitories to night office in the choir – while the station master's office, presiding over Platform 7, the Cambridge platform, was the abbot's lodgings, added on the eve of the Reformation and, indeed, incorporating Tudor Renaissance details in its very pretty façade, now sadly demolished.

It was this ability to find humour and enchantment in absolutely everything which made Alfred's company a constant joy. At that time, for example, most people found Liverpool Street Station a hideous mess. But Alfred loved so many things and approached any activity with such a constant sense of humour, that any event in his company, from the simplest bus journey upwards, was a delight. Indeed, it was on the no. 9 bus, front seat upper deck, that we would set off for the Travellers' Club, the bus always being Alfred's favourite method of transport in London. His critics, that is people who did not know him, supposed him to lead a self-indulgent life of pre-war luxury. Had he wished, he could have done so, as became clear only when the extent of his fortune was revealed on publication of his will. However, he did not enjoy luxury for its own sake, leading a life of planned moderation.

On arrival at the Travellers' we would have lunch, and again, within the context of club life, his tastes were simple: consommé; club claret; well-grilled lamb cutlets from which he carefully removed the inevitable ornamental tomato, a fruit he had no time for; salad, by which he meant nothing but plain lettuce without dressing, 'rabbit food', as he called it; and raspberries when in season, always 'with the cream brought separately', or Stilton. His love of order in all things led him to enjoy rearranging, with long slender fingers, the varied biscuits in piles according to their type and size. He professed not to believe it when I suggested that other members of the club might prefer disordered biscuits rather than those which had received so much attention at his hands. His tastes in food, like much in his life, were the product of his upbringing at Mark Hall where all food was English, fresh, 'off the place', and served without the benefit of continental, or indeed, of any sauces. His enchanting sister Carmen always apologised as she served guests what was, in fact, delicious food, saying, 'It's terribly dry, dear.'

After lunch we might set off on an architectural expedition, or 'promenade archéologique', as he described them in the language of his old friend and mentor Dr Lopes. Notes in my diary remind me of many visits we made, including those to Hampton Court, Osterley, Ham House, Greenwich, and the Tower of London; to churches by Lutyens at Hampstead Garden Suburb, by Beresford Pite at Brixton, and by James Wild at Streatham; to Grange Park, Hampshire, in 1972, weeks before John Baring demolished the wing by Cockerell; to Ireland to stay with Mark Bence- Jones at Glenville Park where we set off for a walk to the lake with Alfred in his frock coat gazing apprehensively at the long grass and confessing, 'I don't want to go through the deep pampas'; to Berlin to stay

with the Scott-Barretts; to Rome with the Knights of Malta; to
Verona for John de Salis's wedding; to Brussels for Roddy Gow's
wedding – here a tiny vignette serves to indicate the fun of being
with Alfred: waiting at Brussels airport, always a tedious pastime,
Alfred was amused by a sign pointing to the 'Escalier de Sauveté',
saying that 'it sounds like an attribute of Our Lady from the Litany
of Loreto'.

At Easter 1969 we made a memorable visit to Spain with Alastair Langlands, staying with Alfred's colourful relatives in Jerez de
la Frontera. At the time, the Labour government had an extraordinarily repressive financial régime which limited the amount of
British currency one could take abroad to an absurd sum like fifty
or a hundred pounds. I remember the astonishment with which
Alastair and I found, as soon as we had been through the passport
control at the airport, that Alfred's clothes were stuffed with hundreds of pounds' worth of bank notes.

Alfred's respect for Franco, then still head of state, was rooted in
memories of the Civil War when his mother would anxiously await
news of the fate of her family and friends at the hands of the Communists. When I asked one of them on this visit for her reminiscences of the war, she spoke of the relief she had felt at news of the
imminent arrival of Franco as 'the forces of order'. Alfred could
also never forget that the entire British media in the 1930s supported the Communists and Republicans. His knowledge of the
Spanish Civil War also did much to explain his hostility to the
British alliance with Stalin during the Second World War, again a
policy scarcely questioned by the media. He told me how Ronald
Knox had asked anxiously at the outbreak of war in 1939, 'Do the
Bishops say it's a just war?' Alfred, by contrast, indifferent as to the
opinion of the Bishops on this topic, was opposed to our fighting
the war at all. He said to me that 'Ronnie was the most old-
fashioned person I have ever known', a view rather at variance with
the image of Knox as a sophisticated figure of immense wit and
irony. Alfred summed him up as 'a Diamond Jubilee Catholic', that
is accepting without question the entire social and political values
of the late Victorian world.

I remember our amusement at finding a menu in a restaurant in Cordova which featured 'over-crusted macaroni', 'kidneys in whisky', and 'goosefish with green sauce', and, by contrast, the dark solemnity of the sacristy of the Encarnación convent below the walls of Avila where St Theresa had been a nun for twenty-seven years. Memories of serving Alfred's Mass in this historic place, so central to Spanish Catholicism, reminds me of the many times when I performed this service throughout England and the Continent. Speaking Spanish, Italian, and French fluently, he was frequently taken for a Spaniard in Spanish sacristies. Serving his Mass involved much patient waiting while Alfred vested and unvested with elaborate precision, following ancient prescriptions which have long since disappeared. We often took with us a chapel case in which everything was packed with meticulous attention to detail, his long fingers smoothing and re-smoothing every item capable of being subdued.

It was the same with his secular packing, if secular is the right word to describe so ritualised a process. He enjoyed the joke of saying, 'Now I will pack while you go and throw a few things into a bag.' As I sat watching him engaged in this process in the guest wing at Downside, he once told me of an identical occasion in the same building, the now demolished White House, when Ronald Knox had witnessed the slow elaborate process of his packing. Seeing his surprise, Alfred explained, 'Ronnie, I have the sort of mind that turned the Last Supper into a pontifical High Mass.' Alfred was amused that he had more than once heard the story told with this phrase attributed to Knox not to him.

His custom in packing was to work every item into its allotted space in the case so that it built up into what he called 'a rich mosaic'. Those who did not know him supposed that these objects were costly and elaborate products of Edwardian masculinity in monogrammed silver, cut-glass, ivory, and embossed leather. Far from it. His worn-down shaving brush was contained within the cardboard cylinder of an ordinary lavatory-paper roll; other items were transported in faded little cardboard boxes; while the favourite containers were the paper bags in which laundries love to return laundered shirts. Continuity and economy were here the order of the day: the same rusting razor with lethal Gillette blades was preserved for decade after decade. Alfred was influenced in all this by reading in John Gore's life of George V that the King Emperor used the same collar stud all his life.

We stayed on a number of occasions in Paris at the Travellers' Club in the Champs-Elysées where Alfred gave parties to promote the career of our dear friend Nicholas Lorriman who had moved to Paris. Alfred enjoyed using the private dining room at the club which in origin had been the Moorish bathroom of the Marquise de Paiva, the *grande horizontale* for whom the house had been built. With the addition of a removable wooden top, her silver-lined bath doubled as a long seat along one side of the table. Alfred also enjoyed the Victorian hydraulic lift which rose in total silence on a glistening iron column, covered with beads of water. It has since been replaced.

We also stayed several times at the château de Chennevières near Paris with Hélène Bourke-Borrowes, who had married an old Essex friend of Alfred's, and her sorrowing niece, Colette d'Amandville, in an atmosphere of Chekhovian decay. Alfred's serenity and lack of worry was borne out by the cheerful lack of attention he gave to picking up the correct suitcase from the carousel at Orly airport. Thus, on arrival at Chennevières he threw it on the bed and, trying to open it, found it was locked, thus showing that it was not his. Monsieur Chemerin, Hélène's hired chauffeur, drove us back to Orly airport where with his characteristic good fortune Alfred's own suitcase awaited him. We discovered that the alien case belonged to a Protestant clergyman from Northern Ireland who, having to change flights in Paris, had been obliged to fly on before it could be retrieved. Alfred feared that this would make him hate the Catholic Church even more and wrote an abject letter of apology for his carelessness.

Back in England, we stayed with Tony Mitchell at Dyrham and with Peter Powis, the bachelor Earl of Powis, at Powis Castle in June 1975. Peter, whom I had first met through Adrian Mathias before he succeeded to the Earldom of Powis in 1974, was by now a prisoner in the hands of his manservant, Edmunds, and his wife, Peter's cook. As a result they made him dine at seven o'clock so that as we rose from dinner at ten to eight, Alfred whispered to me, 'What do we do for the rest of the evening?' In fact we were reduced to doing the *Sunday Express* general knowledge quiz which Peter posted off to the newspaper, enjoying as always the pleasure of giving his name and address as Powis, Powis, Powys, confident that his correct solution would be published over his name the following Sunday. It was not.

A more serious visit was to the Isle of Wight to stay at Quarr Abbey in June 1973 to see the Abbot, Dom Adrian Sillem, who had endeared himself to Alfred by being one of those who, as a young monk at Downside in 1931–34, supported Dom David Knowles in his wish to make Downside more of a contemplative Benedictine community and less a place dominated by the school and compulsory rugby.

By the happiest of chances I spent much of Alfred's last full day on earth with him in Nazareth House nursing home, Hammersmith, to which, increasingly frail, he had moved from the Travellers' Club two months before. He was, as always, contented, having always wanted to be looked after by nuns such as the Poor Sisters of Nazareth at the end of his life. I arrived after breakfast when Alfred, who had already been out to say Mass at the Oratory, had just been shaved by a Spanish barber. I helped him with his second levée, a very long process since he had difficulty in moving his legs, so that getting him into his purple buttoned cassock while he was sitting on the bed was quite a problem. I was also faced with the familiar task of fastening the studs of the clerical collar with its purple stock through the shirt and then passing the loop in the cassock over the back stud.

I gave him a copy of Peter Ackroyd's new biography of Thomas More, one of Alfred's heroes. He wanted to know everything about the author, and I was struck as always by his intense curiosity about people, their life, opinions, and background. I know Peter only slightly but when Alfred assumed he was 'a liberal', I said, 'No, he is a very jolly man and, I imagine, fairly reactionary.' Alfred replied that he meant by the word liberal a modern secularist, that is not a Christian, which I am sure is the case. We sat on the bed looking through every plate in the book which are reproductions of portraits of More and his contemporaries. Alfred, an expert on the iconography of More and Fisher, knew the provenance of every one of them, telling me once again that he doubts whether the Torrigiani bust, formerly at Hatfield Place, Essex, is really an image of St John Fisher.

We had a simple lunch of hospital food with which Alfred was entirely content; the only criticism he could possibly bring himself to make was to say, 'I doubt whether you will care for the ice cream very much.' With it we had a bottle of white Burgundy from Adnam's, the Southwold brewery and wine merchants owned by Simon Loftus, one of a case kindly sent by Simon's mother, Prue, one of Alfred's oldest friends. After lunch, he characteristically insisted on going down to the kitchens to thank the cook, in particular for making an additional lunch for me. The journey was a long one which Alfred performed with great difficulty but great determination, along passages, down the lift, through the hall, and out into the yard. Here we met one of the many sweet nuns who accompanied us into the kitchen and introduced us to a solitary young cook whom Alfred thanked warmly. Though walking, or rather shuffling, with increasing difficulty, Alfred seemed to me to be stronger in other ways since his arrival at Nazareth House where he declared himself to be completely happy. 'I can't think why I didn't come here before,' he said. 'It's like being back in the nursery at Mark Hall.' As I left, two further nuns spoke to me of Alfred with such love, saying he had brought richness to everyone who worked in the place.

Within hours of my leaving him he had a stroke in the night, was given the last sacraments and died peacefully with Sister Brenda holding his hand.

2 · SOME INFLUENCES ON ALFRED

The influence on Alfred of Mark Hall, Harlow, Essex, his home till 1942, was profound, memories of it becoming absolutely central to his emotional life as well as to that of his sister Carmen and his brother Jack, both unmarried. I remember accompanying Alfred in 1971 to Bishop's Stortford Hospital to visit Jack who, though only to be there for a short time, had insisted on taking with him an improbable souvenir of his former family home in the form of an enormous wooden thermometer, the size of a small grandfather clock, which had hung on the garden wall at Mark Hall. He died in 1984 aged ninety-six.

Set in a fine landscaped park by Humphry Repton, Mark Hall was a large and elegant late eighteenth-century country house with much neo-classical plasterwork in the style of James Wyatt. Part of the complex appeal of Mark Hall for Alfred was that, though it seemed the perfect image of timeless Edwardian opulence, it was vulnerable from the start because his father did not own the place but rented it from the Arkwright family from 1893 until his death in 1942, saying that none of his seven children would ever live on that scale. No snob, Alfred was proud of his grandfather who ran a coach between Bishop's Stortford and London, and was fully aware that he was not really born to country house life on this scale.

The same was true of Alfred's hero Hugh Benson, who was conscious of how the appointment of his modestly-born father as Archbishop of Canterbury had promoted his family to life on a truly palatial scale in late Victorian England. It was said of Benson that he could not write a novel in which there was not a second footman. Tethered in the park at Mark Hall was the mediaeval Anglican parish church of St Mary-at-Latton whose vicar, Mr Oliver, would come up to dine with the Gilbey family on Sundays. Alfred remembered him exclaiming on his wife's death in June 1918, 'It's such a snuffing out', which Alfred found an extraordinarily pagan sentiment for an Anglican priest. Alfred recalled that Latton in his boyhood was the perfect parish with virtually no parishioners, save for the head gardener of Mark Hall and his wife who walked up to the church on Sundays from North Lodge. A charming picture of the remoteness of this rural enclave from the modern world, even at that time, is given in the posthumously published autobiography of the musician John Raynor (1909–70),

A Westminster Childhood (1973). Recalling the time when his family stayed with Mr Oliver, two months after his wife's death in 1918, Raynor wrote of evenings when 'the sun had dropped behind a large elm clump, spreading a dusty halo of golden light around the trees, and the fields were sleepy with evening'. He explained that 'Latton vicarage stood in its own park [in fact, that of Mark Hall], and though it was only twenty-two miles from London, it was an old-fashioned place. There was a pony and trap and an old coachman to drive it.'

Life at Mark Hall is recorded in various documents which Alfred preserved carefully: his mothers' diaries, in fact engagement books, from 1899 to her death in 1937; a set of photograph albums which are a marvellous record of country-house life in the years immediately before and after the First World War; and the bound volumes of Alfred's father's letters to his five sons between about 1910 and 1920. Dictated from his office in the Pantheon in Oxford Street from which he ran the family firm, W. & A. Gilbey, these consist of circular letters so that, as Alfred explained, 'One read about oneself in the third person'. They are a remarkable piece of social history, full of information about the day-to-day running of a country house and home farm, and in particular about the varying degrees of success with which pre-war standards were recreated after 1918. I remember especially the account of the problems of arranging the Hunt Ball at Mark Hall in 1919, the first since before the war. His sister Carmen ran Mark Hall up till 1942 so that, as Alfred always put it, 'both my parents were able to die in their beds without ever having known that the social revolution had taken place'.

Alfred's mother was very fond of Dr Doubleday, Bishop of Brentwood, who became a frequent visitor to Mark Hall where, in a bizarre departure from ecclesiastical convention for so cautious and conservative a man, he ordained Alfred in the drawing room in 1929. As a young priest, Alfred was his secretary from 1929 till 1932 when he became chaplain at Cambridge. Alfred recalled with affection his intense conservatism which came close to negativity. A favourite episcopal phrase, often quoted by Alfred, was 'But there won't be time for that this afternoon'. This was on occasions such as confirmation when he would tell children that he ought to give them each a long instruction, but that time ruled it out. His caution meant that he could almost never bring himself to accept any candidate for ordination in his diocese for fear of their going wrong and causing trouble. When once there was a candidate who seemed to Alfred beyond reproach, he asked the Bishop why he had rejected him. 'Too good,' he replied, mournfully.

Dr Doubleday would sometimes ask Alfred to show his guests round the small and ugly Victorian Gothic church, then serving as Brentwood Cathedral, but once had to reprimand him when he heard that, keeping a straight face, Alfred had explained to one visitor that 'Brentwood Cathedral shares with Salisbury the unique distinction of having been built all at one go'.

Two convert clergy, both of whom lived for a time in Cambridge, exercised a powerful influence on Alfred: Monsignor Hugh Benson (1871–1914) and the Rev. Dr John Ludlow Lopes (1880–1960). Though Alfred had loved his Jesuit upbringing at Beaumont, he was never remotely tempted to become a Jesuit himself. His discovery that a priest could operate independently, ordained under his own patrimony, and could look after souls in his own way, came as a revelation to him at the age of fourteen when he read Arthur Benson's book, *Hugh Benson, Memoir of a Brother* (1915). From this he learned that Hugh Benson had been allowed a free rein to operate as a priest, exercising his unique apostolate largely through writing. As an expression of this privilege, Alfred, most unusually, was not ordained in a cathedral or great church but, as we have seen, privately at Mark Hall.

He regretted that he never met Benson but he did meet his brother Arthur, a well-known housemaster at Eton, prolific author, and Master of Magdalene from 1915 to 1925. This meeting took place when Benson came to deliver a literary paper at the Catholic chaplaincy during Alfred's time as an undergraduate at Trinity. He was passionately devoted to Arthur Benson's diary, of which a volume of extracts was published by Percy Lubbock in 1927, as well as to his many books of reminiscences. Alfred shared his love of architecture, his constant humour, and his careful observation of

social nuances and mores. Arthur Benson's books are what Alfred
would have written had he not found writing so difficult. Alfred
was, by contrast, gifted with the most remarkable visual memory
of any man I have ever met, so that with his total visual recall he
could summon up every detail of the settings he so much loved. As
a tiny example, my sister remembers that, having stayed once with
her and her husband at their family home, Chorlton Hall, Cheshire,
on the occasion of his second visit, a decade later, he walked into
the drawing room and remarked immediately, 'You have moved the
position of the bust of Queen Victoria.' Knowing his powers of
observation and memory so well, I did not share my sister's
surprise.

The name of Dr Lopes, Catholic chaplain at Cambridge from
1922 to 1928, including two of the years when Alfred was an
undergraduate, was much on his lips. He spoke to me with constant affection for and devotion to this romantic, flamboyant,
impulsive, Anglo-Catholic convert, who supposedly ran through
two fortunes, being generous to improdigality. Outram Evennett,
Alfred's closest friend at Cambridge until his death aged sixty-three
in 1964, described Alfred as Lopes's 'devoted friend and disciple'.
Wholly impractical, especially in financial affairs, and full of
extravagant schemes, Lopes landed up in the Oxfordshire Bank-
ruptcy Court in April 1929 when it was reckoned that, between his
mother's death in 1912 and 1925, he had spent the immense sum of
between seventy and eighty thousand pounds. In shops where rich
ecclesiastical furnishings were sold, he would exclaim, 'What a
magnificent object, we'll take two of those.'

He was the effective creator of Fisher House, the former Black
Swan public house, overseeing both its purchase in 1924 for the
Cambridge University Catholic Association and also its remodel-
ling by the Birmingham architect, J. Arnold Crush, a name Alfred
always enjoyed. Educated at Exeter College, Oxford, Lopes had
been trained as an Anglican priest at Ely Theological College,
before conversion to the Catholic Church and subsequent training
in Rome where he received a Doctorate in Divinity. He had been an
Anglican curate at the church of St Paul and St Basil's at Deritend in

Birmingham where in about 1910 he had enriched his quarters in the clergy house with expensive oak panelling, designed for him by the aforementioned J. Arnold Crush. This panelling Lopes improbably brought with him to Fisher House where with some inconvenience it was installed for him in the dining room and adjacent sitting room in 1925. Crush's other improvements included the large baldacchino of four Tuscan columns over the altar in the upper chapel at Fisher House. Alfred recalled that Lopes confessed that the columns were not of the solid stone which they appeared to be but were 'Alabaster dust, my dear'. In his diary, Arthur Benson records his meeting with Lopes at which Alfred, as we have noted, was present: 'To the Fisher Society, in mean rooms near the Round Church. Fr. Lopes like a ripe pale plum. I do dislike the RCs, always trying so hard to be like everyone else.'

Lopes's conviviality, independence and originality of outlook, and passionate devotion to the liturgy, 'the solemn worship of Almighty God', to use his and Alfred's favourite phrase, were hugely influential on Alfred's chaplaincy, though Alfred's personal conduct had nothing of Lopes's exuberance. Alfred, characteristically, saw him constantly in his final illness and was with him when he died in September 1960 at St Joseph's Nursing Home in Boars Hill, Oxford.

3 · SOME ASPECTS OF ALFRED'S CHARACTER

Unkindness was a thing Alfred could not bear, the idea of causing offence to anyone causing him enormous distress. He criticised only opinions, never people, a rare exception being Evelyn Waugh whom he found cruel. For someone who read so widely, had so prodigious a memory for literature, and spoke so fluently, it was remarkable that he found writing so painful. Not finding letters a helpful means of communication, he wrote few of them but would rush across the country without a moment's hesitation to see anyone who needed his company. He must have spent as much time at hospital beds, in prisons, and have been present at as many deathbeds as any priest in England, for he put himself wholly and unreservedly at the service, emotional and financial, of anyone who sought his help, making no distinction of manner whatever, regardless of whether he happened to find them congenial or not. Not for nothing was he described in his obituary by Gerard Noel as 'the best-loved priest of his generation'.

He was memorable for his capacity for loyalty and love, for his unwavering devotion to friends and places, and in particular to his homes and places of education: Mark Hall; Beaumont College; Trinity College; the Collegio Beda, Rome; Bishop's House, Brentwood; Fisher House; the Travellers' Club; and even, finally, Nazareth House. He loved them with real passion, whether for their physical beauty, their maintenance of values rejected by the modern world, the enchantment he found in the many friends whom he met in them, or for the idiosyncrasies of their inhabitants which he observed with much affectionate amusement.

I think that what he particularly loved and admired were people and institutions that were true to themselves, for he hated compromise, muddle, and the blurring of distinctions. He thus loved, for example, St John Fisher, St Thomas More, and the 1st Earl of Strafford, making detailed studies of their lives. He also admired the Jewish religion, not being anti-Semitic, as many of his generation were, claiming that he would have been very proud to have been a Jew. He loved, too, the Church of England before the Tractarian movement of the nineteenth century led it to pretend that it was something it was not, part of the Catholic Church. His tutor at Trinity, D. A. Winstanley, to whom he was devoted, used to say, 'My pupil Gilbey admires the worst aspects of the Church of England.' This was the church of Trollope, Alfred's favourite novelist, characterised by parsons' freehold, hunting parsons, and churches with box pews and royal arms. I remember visiting with him two chapels in London, the Charterhouse in 1969 and later Dulwich Old College, where he took pleasure in the survival of low Church, pre-Tractarian, ecclesiastical arrangements and fittings.

Alfred always said that he was 'socially ecumenical but theologically intransigent', so that, with this proviso, he could form close friendships with two Anglican clergymen, F. A. Simpson,

Fellow of Trinity, and Mervyn Stockwood, Vicar of Great St Mary's, Cambridge, and subsequently Bishop of Southwark. Forming one of the more improbable aspects of Alfred's purely social ecumenism, this association flowered annually in the form of a lavish dinner for a small number of friends which he gave in Simpson's honour on, as he put it, 'the date closest to the Feast of St Cecilia that is convenient to the Bishop of Southwark', that feast-day, 22 November, being the date of Simpson's birth in 1883. This is not the place to describe Simpson, Alfred's supervisor in History as an undergraduate at Trinity, other than to say that he was perhaps the most eccentric Fellow that great college has ever nurtured. But he was also a master of English prose, both spoken and written, and was an endless source of entertainment to Alfred. A man of exceptional nervous delicacy, it was recorded that as a young curate in Cumberland around 1905 he visited his humbler parishioners wearing a muslin respirator to ward off any noxious effluvia they might emit.

I saw much of Simpson before his death in 1974 at the age of ninety and was present at a number of the birthday dinners which Alfred gave for him each year. Harry Williams, former Dean of Trinity, as well as Mervyn Stockwood, were usually present at these when there would typically be reminiscences of what in the years before and after the First World War used to be called 'mixed bathing', or friendly relations between Anglo-Catholics and Roman Catholics. There was also much talk of a novel which emerged from that world called *Peradventure, or the Silence of God* (1922), by Robert Keable, of which Alfred gave me a copy in 1966.

Mervyn Stockwood bullied Simpson intolerably about past friendships and his religious position. I can hear him now, loudly addressing the frail old man as 'Simbo', an inappropriate though presumably affectionate nickname for someone whom I heard no one else, not even Alfred, address to his face as anything other than Simpson. In his absence he was always referred to as 'Mr Simpson', just as his arch-enemy at Trinity, the classicist Andrew Gow, was 'Mr Gow'. Alfred's friendship with Mervyn Stockwood, a loud, booming figure who was an overtly homosexual socialist, was superficially puzzling, but one reason for his association with Mervyn was that he never rejected anyone who sought his company and treated everyone with equal warmth. Mervyn had approached him, on his arrival at Great St Mary's in 1955, for advice on the design of vestments which he wished to introduce into his services. They were not common then or now in college chapels, so that it was reasonable for him to turn for advice to the Catholic chaplain rather than to a college chaplain. As a result, the first vestments used in Great St Mary's since the Reformation were planned using paper models cut out on the floor of the Great Chamber at Fisher House.

Another link was that Mervyn was a fervent admirer of Simpson, hence the dinners already referred to. Alfred, like Simpson, had a passionate devotion to Trinity College. He dined there regularly, as had Dr Lopes, observing the idiosyncrasies of the Fellows with great joy. I once asked Alfred whether he had met Goodhart-Rendel, a Trinity man and an architect and critic whom I much admire. 'Yes,' he said, 'at Cambridge in 1946 at the four-hundredth anniversary celebrations of the founding of Trinity College.' Also present were George VI and Queen Elizabeth who were forced to watch an eighteenth-century cricket match being played on the Trinity Paddocks. Alfred was a connoisseur of the entertainments which the Fellows of Trinity suppose will amuse visiting royalty. He remembered a visit to the college of Edward VIII as Prince of Wales, and the look of polite boredom on his face as he watched, of all things, a display of Morris dancing on the lawn in Nevile's Court.

He delighted in the precise enunciation of Harry Hollond, Fellow in Law at Trinity, who was born in 1883 and lived to be ninety. Hollond gave an equal stress to every syllable, and almost every word, including the definite article, with a slight pause between the words. The reason was, as Alfred put it, imitating his careful manner of speaking, 'Professor Hollond had el-o-cut-ion lessons at the age of eighteen and has never got over them'. He remembered Hollond telling a story of how he and his wife, Marjorie, saw 'an extraordinary thing' on their holiday in some Mediterranean country: 'the village women', Hollond explained, 'did their washing in the river and afterwards laid the clothes out on the stones to dry.' Alfred was entertained by this as evidence of the remoteness from the outer world of the Fellows of Trinity of Hollond's day, for, as Alfred explained, 'probably the majority of women in the world did their washing in this way, but to a product of the Trinity of Hollond's generation, it offered an exciting glimpse into a primitive world.'

Sitting in the Parlour at Trinity before dinner one evening, I once heard Hollond come in with a foreign guest to whom he announced, 'We call this room the Parlour.' His careful, balanced enunciation lent an indefinable air of detachment, almost disdain, to this statement, as though the real name of the room were different and possibly more interesting, but that for some long forgotten or faintly discreditable reason the anodyne name 'Parlour' had been adopted. Alfred enormously enjoyed the phrase, 'We call this room the Parlour', which became one of our many little private jokes.

Practical jokes, too, were dear to Alfred, particularly in his younger years before I knew him. They were very much part of Edwardian country house life, Alfred's older brothers mercilessly teasing their tutor, a German called Carl Bogler. Alfred's friend Alfonso de Zulueta, parish priest at Holy Redeemer, Cheyne Row, had a sentimental regard for animals, rare in a Spaniard – he was even prepared to bless them. Alfred accordingly wrote him a letter purporting to be from someone who wanted him to devote a whole service to this purpose at which a wide range of animals from domestic pets to donkeys would be blessed, not *in absentia*, but live: they would actually be brought into the church. Alfonso fell for the whole thing.

Then there was Outram Evennett's elephant. Outram, Alfred's close friend, was a Fellow of Trinity of a retiring and slightly nervous disposition. Hearing that Bertram Mills' s circus was to be in town, Alfred conducted a correspondence with its manager, purportedly on Outram's behalf, in the hope of persuading him to lend an elephant to Trinity College as part of a fund-raising event for charity. Unfortunately, Outram was less gullible than Alfonso de

Zulueta, so the scene which Alfred envisaged never took place at which the college porters would ring up an unsuspecting Outram in his rooms and announce, 'Mr Evennett, sir, your elephant's arrived. Shall we send it round?'

A far smaller but more successful animal trick which Alfred played on me was to put an enormous stuffed spider in my bed when we were staying with Sherman and Jeanne Camoys at Stonor Park. He had removed it from a glass case in a downstairs passage in which Sherman housed a large collection of these horrible things which, professionally stuffed, were alarmingly realistic, especially for someone like myself who has an absurd fear of spiders.

I was present at a dinner party in 1977 at which Alfred played another little practical joke. At this dinner, which he gave in a private room in Buck's Club in honour of Robin McDouall, the Secretary of the Travellers' Club, the other guests were Alfred's nephew Mark, his old friend from school, Count Tony Mattei, and a young member of the Travellers' called Nigel Muers-Raby. A rather peppery man but a distinguished gourmet and author of numerous books and articles on food, Robin had retired two or three years earlier from being a brilliant Secretary of the Travellers' Club for twenty-nine years.

It was entirely thanks to Robin's support that Alfred was able to secure his permanent room in the club, but he thought that this evening would he a good time to play a mild practical joke on him. He asked me to write out a spoof menu for which we invented unpromising courses including mushroom soup, liver as the main dish, and sardines as the savoury. I can hear Robin now, asking 'What goodies have you got for me?' as he entered the little panelled room and inspected the menu. His face did not fall at all and Alfred congratulated him on being the perfect gentleman as he handed him the real menu with smoked salmon, pheasant, and canapé Diane.

Robin, like all of Alfred's friends, was, as I find I keep on repeating, an endless source of amusement to him. Alfred also said that if one happened to mention a grand acquaintance to Robin, say a duchess, he would ask, incredulously, 'How do you know her?' But if he, by contrast, mentioned a similar connection whom one had not met, he would say, 'Oh, don't you know her?' So one could never win.

Alfred's life at the Travellers' involved his ritualisation of processes such as packing, retiring, rising, and dressing. The leisurely pace at which these activities were conducted considerably slowed down his life but perhaps, in the end, helped extend it by eliminating unnecessary rush and strain. He was a perfectionist in clothes. His nightshirts, made for him by New and Lingwood, had to incorporate a particular kind of blue embroidered border in a Greek key pattern. When this became difficult to find, it had to be transferred from an old nightshirt to a new one. He also regretted that it became virtually impossible to have stiff collars and cuffs properly laundered, while his favourite grey suede gloves also seemed to become unavailable. This made his frequent bus journeys less enjoyable, for he had always refused to touch the greasy pole by the entrance with his bare hand.

For many years he carried his Truslove and Hanson visiting cards in an elegant silver case, delicately curved to fit the ribs so that it fitted neatly into his waistcoat pocket. It caught the attention of James Lees-Milne who came to dine when Alfred was staying with Elizabeth Wansbrough at Broughton Poggs in 1972. Lees-Milne wrote a charming description of Alfred in his diary as 'well groomed and well dressed in clerical togs and a sort of mourning coat. He has a silver calling-card case in his pocket; is entertaining, likes heraldry and gossip. Is bright and good company.' I read this to Alfred when James Lees-Milne published it in *A Mingled Measure* in 1994, but he said he had lost the case years ago and never replaced it.

Until the introduction of the hated decimal coinage another ritualised part of Alfred's private life was his custom of carrying eight half-crowns with him. The ritual of his retiring at night was considerably prolonged by the process in which he washed these coins at the end of each day, having gone through his small change selecting coins with images of Kings George V and VI in preference to those of Elizabeth II whose face on the coinage he described at this time,

with affection not disdain, as that of 'a pert girl'. This cleaning
process he found a reassuring echo of Edwardian England when servants washed small change and ironed newspapers and bootlaces.

His indulgence each morning in what he called his 'first and
second levées', seemingly a survival of the court of Louis XIV
rather than that of Edward VII, might be said to have slowed down
his life to an undesirable extent. The justification for it was that he
rose early at six every day of his life from his time as a student at the
Beda. He then said Mass for which, during his life in London, he
had to travel across west London to the Oratory, not returning to
the club till half past eight. He then had a leisurely breakfast which
daily included two poached eggs and latterly, in addition, an enormous quantity of prunes which were subjected, once de-stoned, to
a ritual process, being arranged in pairs round the edge of the plate.
After this, *The Times* was consulted for births, marriages, and
deaths.

Then at about half past nine the second levée took place. All the
clothes came off, a complicated process in itself for many a strap
passed through many a toggle. Then a thorough wash or bath and a
clean shirt and underwear. He then read his office in the chapel
after which, typically, a guest would arrive for lunch. It will be seen
that the normal part of a man's day when he might be supposed to
deal with his correspondence, say between nine and eleven, was
thus neatly removed from Alfred's day. He hated dealing with business or writing letters, even to close friends, and the 'second levée'
seemed to have been invented, perhaps unconsciously to fill the
time legitimately. He was conscious of his inability to deal effectively with business matters or to answer correspondence: indeed,
he once confessed that 'this has ruined my life'.

Part of his reluctance to introduce changes into his daily routine,
a reluctance which naturally became greater as he grew older,
meant that for the whole of his life, long after his family had left
Harlow on his father's death in 1942, he kept his substantial bank
account at the modest branch of Barclay's Bank, Station Road,
Harlow, never moving it to Cambridge or London. Always aiming
at private modesty, despite his generosity to others, he used to

restrict himself at Cambridge in the 1960s to withdrawing only £5 at a time from his account. I remember going with him on one occasion to the Bene't Street branch of Barclay's, the closest to Fisher House. The cashier, noting that his account was not in Cambridge but in Harlow, asked him, 'Do you have an arrangement?' Explaining to her that he had, he whispered to me, 'It's like asking, "Do you have a truss?"'

The Travellers', of course, was far from being his only club. He had long been a member of the Athenaeum, for which his father had put him up as a very young man, of Buck's, of which his brother Charles had been a founder member, of Pratt's, of which its proprietor, the Duke of Devonshire made him a member, of the Beefsteak, where I had the honour of proposing him, and, in Cambridge of the Pitt Club and the Strafford Club, the latter being a dining club which he and a group of friends had founded in March 1939.

At the Athenaeum, not given over to high living, there was a time in the 1960s when club servants created the impression that dinner in the Coffee Room was definitely at an end at some point between half past eight and nine. There was a sense of chairs being stacked on tables, of surfaces swabbed down. At just this point, Alfred once asked the exhausted old Irish waitress whether, if she could find one, he could have 'a really nice ripe Cox's apple'. As she set back on the long journey to the kitchen exit at the far end of the vast Coffee Room, he heard her mutter under her breath, 'Jesus, I could scream!' He always sympathised with the wish of these harassed ladies to 'catch the last bus back to Hornsey Rise', as he put it.

The Athenaeum was an endless source of entertainment to him. As long as he, and I, belonged to it, the menu contained the discouraging item, 'Arbroath Smokies, when available'. Another delight was the door of the Billiard Room through which one passed to gain access to the subterranean Ladies' Annexe, much used by Alfred for entertaining mixed parties. The door bore the menacing notice, 'Wait for the shot'. Nearby, was a deliciously cool lobby containing a complete set of bound volumes of *Punch*. Perusal of these was a favourite pastime of Alfred, especially in the

summer when he found the chill temperature of the lobby especially welcome. Despite his Spanish blood, he was, as he was the
first to admit, physically ill adapted to heat.

Given his devotion to the Athenaeum, his decision to resign in
1977 on a matter of principle was a source of sadness to him. He
had proposed as a member a young friend, a former member of his
flock in Cambridge, who was rejected by the election committee on
the grounds that he had not yet reached a sufficiently high grade in
the civil service. Alfred was appalled at the consequent implication
that the club had ceased to be a gentlemen's club but was now some
sort of professional association. He argued that, if it had been that
in the 1920s, he would never have been elected himself. He conducted a protracted correspondence with the Secretary and the
Chairman, and when they refused to give way, resigned with enormous reluctance. When, in the 1970s so many clubs were forced to
close, following inflation caused by the oil crisis, he used to say
that, 'The Athenaeum will always survive as the canteen of the
establishment.'

4 · A CAMBRIDGE FOOTNOTE

I will end in Cambridge, the place which had brought Alfred and
me together in the first place. He once recalled that, on his return to
Cambridge as chaplain in 1932, he made Tuesday, his servants' day
off, his own day off too. In one of his very rare published articles, in
The Field in 1985, he described one of these Tuesdays in a manner
which makes one regret that he could not be persuaded to write
more often:

> I would go out with the beagles, I would drink tea at the Pitt, I
> would dine in Trinity and I would go up afterwards to the
> Combination Room to drink wine. On one such occasion I
> found myself sitting in hall next to an international jurist of
> world-wide repute. I felt it incumbent on me to explain what
> someone as undistinguished himself as myself was doing in
> such distinguished company. When I told him that I was

taking my day off and recounted how I had spent the afternoon and was spending the evening, he replied with great gravity, 'I have no doubt that you have given your mind to the moral problems involved, and have solved them to your satisfaction.' I replied 'Entirely.' Whether he was satisfied I shall never know but I am confident that I shall carry the readers of *The Field* with me.

After leaving Fisher House in 1965, he kept his beagling clothes, including a waistcoat sporting the Essex Hunt Club buttons of his youth, in the rooms in Magdalene of an enchanting Fellow of that college, Dick Ladborough. After Dick's death in 1972, the beagling gear was transferred to my rooms in Peterhouse where Alfred always changed and drank sherry before setting off with the hounds.

For all but three of our long years of friendship, he was what is officially called a non-resident member of the university. He had persuaded himself that the correct dress for a non-resident M.A. on his return visits to Cambridge was a gown and a top hat. He and his old Trinity friend, Geoffrey Lloyd, had, indeed, found a Victorian university regulation that a returning M.A. should wear a silk hat, i.e. top hat, rather than a square, i.e. mortar board, though it seemed to me that the sense of this was that he should wear in Cambridge whatever headgear he would normally wear on formal occasions outside the university, and that this would necessarily change as one century gave way to another. But change was not Alfred's favourite thing in life, so a top hat it had to be. He kept one in London for weddings, funerals, and memorial services, and one in Cambridge which he wore on formal occasions, largely restricted to the memorial services of Fellows of Trinity which he and I attended together in the college chapel, including those of Harry Hollond, Simpson, Patrick Duff, Walter Ullmann, Kitson Clark, and, in 1990, the last, that of Tressilian Nicholas who had died aged 101.

The precious hat was guarded between Alfred's visits to Cambridge by Mr Bays, of Bays and Son, in King's Parade, an old-fashioned shirt-makers later bought by New and Lingwood, and now sadly closed down. On the morning of an imminent visit, I would telephone Mr Bays to warn him so that he could bring the hat up from his cellar and polish it. After arrival at the station, Alfred would then call at my rooms in Peterhouse for lunch after which we would collect the hat from Mr Bays and walk on to Trinity. Sometimes he would stay on so that we could dine together in Trinity where his silk M.A. gown was kept for him in the lodge by the porters who always took an age to find it.

The day after Alfred died, I dined in Trinity and performed the melancholy task of retrieving his gown for the last time. Of course, no Fellows seemed concerned by his death, but that is exactly what he would have expected: colleges are always being reborn and do not mourn. After dinner, I strolled through Nevile's Court and down to the river, as I had so often with Alfred. Holding his gown close to me, I gazed with misted eyes at the view from Trinity Bridge towards the pinnacled skyline of St John's where the golden lights winking from the mullioned windows below were darkly reflected in the still Cam. It is one of the most poetic views in England and was as dear to Alfred as anything on earth.